ITALIAN LIGHT COOKING

ITALIAN LIGHT COOKING

By Marie Simmons

A JOHN BOSWELL ASSOCIATES/KING HILL PRODUCTIONS BOOK

A PERIGEE BOOK

Perigee Books
are published by
The Putnam Publishing Group
200 Madison Avenue
New York, NY 10016

Published simultaneously in Canada

Library of Congress Cataloging-in-Publication Data

Simmons, Marie
Italian light cooking / Marie Simmons.
p. cm.
Includes index.
ISBB 0-399-51740-5 (trade pbk.)
1. Cookery, Italian. I. Title.
TX723.S49 1992 91-38261 CIP
641.5945—dc20

Design by Nan Jernigan/The Colman Press
Cover illustration and design by Richard Rossiter
Printed in the United States of America
1 2 3 4 5 6 7 8 9 10

This book is printed on acid-free paper.

Special thanks to my neighbors—taste testers
par excellence:
Ted, Betsy, Heide, Geoff, Lynda, Ray
and
John, the best taste tester of all.

CONTENTS

Introduction

Contrary to what some Americans think, Italian food is not the stereotypical mountain of spaghetti crowned with baseball-sized meatballs and a plate of sticky sweet pastries stuffed with gooey cream. In fact, if we were to step into a kitchen in the Tuscan countryside or in a small restaurant in a Roman *piazza,* we might see a table spread with tomatoes stuffed with rice salad, a small veal roast and a side dish of braised escarole served with lemon wedges—appealing, lean and nutritious fare. For dessert, there might well be sweet ripe cherries, served simply in a bowl of iced water. The mound of spaghetti is an Italian-American creation and the sweet pastries are only served alongside espresso, for a midmorning or afternoon snack, much as we might have coffee and a doughnut.

Real Italian food, by its very nature, is inherently healthful. Light and fresh, it reflects many of the most up-to-date guidelines for good nutrition. The keystones of Italian cuisine include vegetables, fruits, grains, poultry and seafood, with relatively small amounts of red meat. Favorite Italian foods like pasta, rice, bread, potatoes and beans, which are naturally high in complex carbohydrates, also provide essential nutrients like vitamins, protein, minerals and dietary fiber.

In southern Italian cooking, olive oil is the preferred fat, while in the north cooks use butter. While the number of calories per tablespoon is the same for all fats, in this book I have chosen to cook only with olive oil, since its high monosaturated fat ratio makes it about the healthiest fat you can use. I've kept the amounts of all fats to a minimum.

In fact, eating more carbohydrates, significantly less fat and moderate amounts of protein, which current studies suggest as the most nutritious diet you can follow, has a wonderful side benefit: reduced calorie consumption. That's because fats contain an incredibly dense number of calories per gram—more than twice as much as any other type of food. Rather than counting individual calories, many doctors recommend just cutting fats. It's simpler and takes far less work. In *Italian Light Cooking,* the recipes espouse both alternatives: They were developed using a minimum of fat, *and* the calories have been counted for you.

When you leaf through this book, I think you'll see how pleasant and light Italian cooking can be. If you concentrate on seafood, poultry, plenty of vegetables and fresh fruit, consume dairy products and red meat in moderation and improve your diet of complex carbohydrates, you are bound for healthier eating. That's the Italian table. Research has even shown that the people living in Italy and other Mediterranean countries, who have spent their lifetimes eating this type of diet, have a lower incidence of coronary heart disease.

The food of Italy, long admired for its imagination, freshness, simplicity and good taste, easily answers the needs of the health-conscious American consumer who is looking for a dietary plan appropriate to a demanding contemporary lifestyle without any sacrifice of good taste.

Ingredients in the Italian Kitchen

OLIVE OIL—Olive oil is the cornerstone of Italian cuisine. Supermarkets now stock a variety of moderately priced olive oils—both extra virgin and Zpure. The difference between extra virgin and pure olive oil is the taste. Extra virgin olive oil has a distinct olive flavor, and it will add an enormous amount of flavor to your cooking. Use it in salads, as a marinade or as a condiment. There is nothing quite like the taste of a perfectly ripe tomato drizzled with a little extra virgin olive oil.

For most cooking and sautéing, however, the flavor of extra virgin olive oil would be lost, so it's not worth the extra expense. Pure olive oil has a relatively neutral or bland taste, is less expensive and is perfectly appropriate for cooking or whenever you prefer a more "invisible" oil.

A product called light olive oil is pure olive oil with all of the flavor removed and was developed especially for the American consumer who wants the health benefits of a monounsaturated oil without a strong olive taste.

Selecting a bottle of olive oil can be confusing. Purchase the smallest size of two different brands, and when you decide which one you prefer, buy the larger, more economical size. Store in a cool dark place, below the counter kitchen cabinet, for example. An opened bottle of olive oil should stay fresh for about one year, but hopefully you will use it up sooner than that. If olive oil is stored in the refrigerator, it will become cloudy, but that in no way affects the flavor or quality. Let the bottle stand at room temperature for a little while, and it will clear up.

PARMESAN CHEESE—Parmigiano-Reggiano is the most revered of the Italian cheeses. It is made from cow's milk in a specifically designated region of northern Italy. Aged for a minimum of two years, the words "Parmigiano-Reggiano" are stamped in red on the rind. The flavor is nutty and rich, with a very mild salt edge. Although other good-tasting Parmesan cheeses are made throughout the world, none is as distinctive as the real thing.

Whatever type of Parmesan you use, for optimum flavor and freshness, it pays to buy a wedge of cheese rather than a container that is already grated. Grated cheese loses its flavor quickly and when watching calories, it makes sense to use a small amount of cheese with a lot of flavor rather than additional cheese—and more fat—to compensate for lack of flavor.

MOZZARELLA CHEESE—There are basically two types of mozzarella cheese. The first type, available in every supermarket, is the factory-made or processed mozzarella, which is now available as whole milk, part-skim, reduced-fat and fat-free (see calorie chart on p. 154). This type of aged mozzarella is a perfect melting cheese, which makes it so popular as a topping on hot dishes like pizza.

The second type is called fresh mozzarella. The true Italian mozzarella is made from water buffalo milk, but because it is highly perishable (and extremely expensive), it is rarely found in this country. In some areas, local Italian groceries or cheese stores make their own fresh mozzarella from cow's milk. Tender and sweet-tasting, with a slightly chewy texture, fresh cow's milk mozzarella should be used in salads or dishes where the cheese is not heated. This type of mozzarella does not melt well.

Commercially made fresh mozzarella, sold in three sizes and packed in tubs of water, are now available in many supermarkets. Look for them in the refrigerated dairy case or in the deli section of your market. Sizes, ranging from small to large, are *ciliegine,* or "little cherries," *bocconcini,* or "bite size," and *ovoline,* or "egg shaped."

TOMATOES—The only time to enjoy fresh tomatoes is at the height of the tomato season. The flavor of a vine-ripened tomato still warm from the sun is unsurpassed. Never refrigerate a fresh uncut tomato; it dulls the taste. Out of season, it's better—and much less expensive—to use canned tomatoes rather than try to coax flavor from the hard, pink tomatoes available that have never properly ripened.

Excellent-quality canned tomatoes are sold in most markets. Try out different brands until you find the one that you prefer. I like the flavor and texture of imported canned Italian-style plum tomatoes best.

HERBS—Fresh herbs provide a great way to add extra flavor to a dish that has had its calories reduced by incorporating less fat. Many supermarkets now sell small packages of fresh herbs. These will keep fresh for at least a week if you refrigerate them in a small glass of water and cover it with a plastic bag. A much more economical alternative is to buy small herb plants at a garden center and plant them in pots, window boxes or in your garden. Fresh basil and parsley—two very popular herbs in this collection of recipes—are prolific, easy-growing herbs. It's fun to be able to walk outside or reach out a city kitchen window and snip a few leaves of basil for the evening's salad.

Dried herbs are also a good way to add flavor, but because the flavor is more intense, they should be used sparingly. Too much of a dried herb can turn a dish bitter. Most of the following recipes call for ¼ teaspoon of a dried herb; rarely do I use more. Dried herbs do lose their flavor if stored for long periods of time. If dried herbs are more than a year old or if they've lost their bright green color and fragrant aroma, they should be discarded and replaced with a fresh supply.

A good trick for reconstituting a dried herb is to finely chop it along with a sprig of fresh parsley. The parsley juice mingles with the dried herb, giving it a new lease on flavor.

GARLIC—Look for garlic with loose papery skin; the cloves should be juicy and sweet smelling when you cut into them. A new crop of garlic arrives in most stores every spring and summer. Winter garlic is usually stronger because it has been stored. Keep garlic in a cool, dry place in a container that allows air to circulate around it. I use a small earthenware pot without a lid; my mother always stored her garlic in a glass jar without a top. Garlic that has sprouted will have a much stronger flavor and should be discarded. If you suddenly find yourself with a whole jar full of sprouted garlic, separate the cloves and retrieve the ones without visible sprouts. Halve them and cut out the small green sprout that may be beginning to grow within the clove; these tend to be bitter.

Most people do not have the patience or dexterity to mince a clove of garlic with the precision of a chef, which is why many of the following recipes call for garlic crushed through a press. I prefer not to use garlic that has been prechopped and stored in oil. If you do use this type, it is imperative that it be stored in the refrigerator after it has been opened, or harmful bacteria can develop.

CHICKEN BROTH—I use either homemade chicken broth without added salt or canned unsalted or reduced-sodium broth in the following recipes. To minimize calories, fat and cholesterol, make sure to skim the small globs of fat floating on top of the canned broth. There are almost 2 cups of broth in a 14½-ounce can. If you pour directly from the can rather than pouring it first into a measuring cup, the fat will fall to the bottom of the can. If you use reduced-sodium broth instead of the unsalted broth, taste the dish first before adding any additional salt.

BREAD CRUMBS—When a recipe calls for fine dry bread crumbs, I am using the type available in the cylindrical box in the bread section of your supermarket. When I call for coarse dry bread crumbs from day-old Italian bread, I am referring to only slightly dry coarse crumbs that I make myself from stale bread. If you think of it, either make the crumbs ahead and freeze them until needed, or freeze the bread when you have it on hand, then thaw it and make the crumbs as they are needed.

This is how to make coarse crumbs from day-old Italian bread: With a large knife, slice the bread into ¼-inch slices, then cut each slice into narrow strips. Chop the narrow strips into small pieces. Then, if the bread isn't too dry, it can be crumbled with your fingers into coarse crumbs or you can pulverize it in a food processor. If the bread is very dry, it will need to be "crumbled" by being cut with a large knife.

Chapter One

ANTIPASTI

In Italian, *anti* means "before" and *pasto* (the singular of *pasti*) means "meal." Thus, the word *antipasto* literally means "before the meal." In a traditional multicourse Italian meal, the antipasto is served first, followed by a soup and/or pasta and then the meat or fish course. An antipasto can be as simple as a dish of olives or marinated carrots, or as elaborate as an assortment of grilled vegetables, seafood salads, sliced sausages and salamis, breads and cheese.

When dining out in Italy, it is easy to compose a meal entirely from antipasto dishes. Often an entire wall of a restaurant will be devoted to a long table laden with dozens of irresistibly colorful, enticing-looking dishes from which to choose.

In this country, too, the trend toward sampling a number of smaller dishes has become popular, and often the appetizers look like the most appealing part of the menu. Happily, in Italian cooking, these wholesome dishes lean heavily toward vegetables, which makes them particularly appropriate for those of us who are watching fat, cholesterol and calories. Many of the dishes are marinated or pickled, so they have vibrant flavors that are especially satisfying. The main trick is to learn to cook with less olive oil—the primary source of fat in Italian food. Many of these zesty and bite-size dishes, such as the Black Olives Marinated with Lemon and Herbs or the Mushroom Crostini, make excellent hot and cold appetizers and hors d'oeuvres.

The following antipasti recipes are an excellent introduction to what Italian food is all about. High in complex carbohydrates and low in fat, antipasti are delicious, simple to prepare and attractive. And they provide nutritious fare. Ricotta, Lemon and Basil Dip with Assorted Vegetables, Fresh Mozzarella Salad with Tomatoes and Basil, Baked Stuffed Mushroom Caps and Baked Rolled Stuffed Eggplant with a light tomato sauce are just a few of the lean treats you'll find in this chapter. For further antipasto ideas, look also in the vegetable chapter. Many of these side-dish recipes, particularly the marinated vegetables, are right at home on the antipasto plate, as are the seafood salads that appear at the end of Chapter 6.

Choose a single antipasto recipe as an appetizer, present an assortment of dishes to a larger group as a first course or set out a buffet selection as a lunch or light supper. Because the counts are so low—all 200 calories or less and many well below 100—you can afford to splurge. Indulge yourself with an extra portion of your favorite dish, or perhaps a slice of Crostini (p. 21), Italian garlic toast, to sop up the juices from one of the marinated vegetables.

Pinzimonio

Crisp, raw vegetables are a dieter's salvation, which some Italians turn into a dish that's pretty to serve and tasty and fun to eat. *Pinzimonio,* from the Italian word meaning "to pinch or grasp," is a beautiful display of well-chilled, crunchy fresh vegetables that are picked up with the fingers, then dipped in a simple selection of seasonings: extra virgin olive oil, coarse salt, freshly ground pepper and, occasionally, red wine vinegar.

6 Servings | 158 Calories per serving

¾ pound fennel bulb, trimmed of tough outer stalk and fernlike tops and thickly sliced
8 celery rib hearts with their leafy tops, trimmed and quartered
12 thin scallions, roots and tough tops trimmed
18 baby carrots, scrubbed, or 3 small carrots, peeled and cut into 2-inch lengths
18 small radishes with tops, rinsed, outer leaves trimmed
1 head of radicchio, separated into leaves
2 heads of Belgian endive, separated into leaves
⅓ cup extra virgin olive oil
¼ cup red wine vinegar
Coarse salt and freshly ground black pepper

1. Soak the fennel, celery, scallions, carrots and radishes in a large bowl of ice water 20 minutes to crisp before using. Drain well.

2. Arrange all the vegetables decoratively in a shallow bowl or basket or on a platter. Pass the olive oil, red wine vinegar, coarse salt and a pepper mill.

Bruschetta

Yes, you can afford bread when you are eating lean, if it is portioned judiciously and prepared without other high-fat ingredients. This simple appetizer is a special treat during the height of the summer season, when both vine-ripened tomatoes and fresh basil are at their peak. Buy the best Italian bread available, preferably whole wheat, the sweetest plum tomatoes and a flavorful extra virgin olive oil. For an authentic Italian taste, toast the bread over a grill; in Italy a wood fire is used.

20 Slices, 10 Servings — 112 Calories per serving

20 slices of Italian bread, cut ½ inch thick
1 small garlic clove, halved
¼ cup extra virgin olive oil
1 to 1½ cups diced ripe tomatoes
1 tablespoon finely chopped red onion
20 small basil leaves or torn pieces of larger basil leaves
Coarse salt

1. Light a hot fire in your grill or preheat your broiler.

2. Lightly rub one side of each slice of bread with the cut side of the garlic. Brush each slice lightly with a scant ½ teaspoon olive oil. Grill the bread until lightly toasted on both sides, 1 to 2 minutes.

3. In a small bowl, combine the tomatoes, onion and remaining olive oil. Toss to mix.

4. Arrange the toasts on a platter. Place a small basil leaf or a piece of leaf on each slice. Top with a spoonful of the tomato mixture. Serve the bruschetta with a small dish of coarse salt passed on the side, so guests can season the toasts to their taste.

Crostini

Crostini are basically Italian croutons, or garlic toasts, made from slices of Italian bread. They are delicious eaten in a variety of ways: floated in soup, spread with a savory purée, covered with a film of melted cheese or diced and tossed in salads.

24 Slices, 12 Servings — 95 Calories per serving

¼ cup olive oil
1 garlic clove, crushed through a press
24 slices of Italian bread, cut ½ inch thick

1. Preheat the oven to 350° F. Combine the olive oil and garlic in a small bowl. With a pastry brush, lightly brush the garlic oil over one side of each bread slice. Arrange the slices in a single layer on a large baking sheet.

2. Bake 10 minutes. Turn the bread over and bake until the slices are golden, about 10 to 15 minutes longer. Let cool on a wire rack or serve warm.

Parmesan Crostini

24 Slices, 12 Servings — 132 Calories per serving

¼ cup olive oil
1 garlic clove, crushed through a press
24 slices of Italian bread, cut ½ inch thick
4 ounces Parmesan cheese, grated (1 cup)

1. Preheat the oven to 400° F. Combine the olive oil and garlic in a small bowl. With a pastry brush, lightly brush the garlic oil over one side of each bread slice. Arrange the slices in a single layer on a large baking sheet.

2. Bake 10 minutes. Remove the baking sheet from the oven. Turn the bread over. Sprinkle a heaping tablespoon grated Parmesan cheese on each slice of bread.

3. Return to the oven and bake the slices until the cheese is melted and the bread is golden, 10 to 15 minutes longer. Serve warm.

Mushroom Crostini

24 Slices, 12 Servings 111 Calories per serving

¼ cup plus 1 tablespoon olive oil
2 garlic cloves, crushed through a press
24 slices of Italian bread, cut ½ inch thick
½ pound white button mushrooms, thinly sliced (about 2 cups)
2 tablespoons chopped onion
1 tablespoon finely chopped Italian (flat leaf) parsley
⅛ teaspoon salt
Freshly ground black pepper

1. Preheat the oven to 400° F. Combine ¼ cup of the olive oil and 1 of the crushed garlic cloves in a small bowl. With a pastry brush, lightly brush the garlic oil over one side of each bread slice. Arrange the slices in a single layer on a large baking sheet.

2. Bake 10 minutes. Turn the bread over and bake until the slices are golden, 10 to 15 minutes longer. Let cool on a wire rack.

3. In a large nonstick skillet, heat the remaining 1 tablespoon olive oil over medium heat. Add the mushrooms and onion and cook over medium-high heat, stirring, until the mushrooms are lightly browned, about 10 minutes. Add the remaining garlic and the parsley. Cook 1 minute longer. Add the salt and a grinding of pepper. Let cool slightly.

4. Spoon about ½ tablespoon of the mushroom mixture onto each toasted slice of bread. Serve warm or at room temperature.

Rosemary Crostini

24 Slices, 12 Servings 96 Calories per serving

¼ cup olive oil
1 garlic clove, crushed through a press
24 slices of Italian bread, cut ½ inch thick
1 tablespoon dried rosemary

1. Preheat the oven to 350° F. Combine the olive oil and garlic in a small bowl. With a pastry brush, lightly brush the garlic oil over one side of each bread slice. Arrange the slices in a single layer on a large baking sheet. Sprinkle the rosemary evenly over the bread.

2. Bake 10 minutes. Turn the bread over and bake until the slices are golden, about 10 to 15 minutes longer. Let cool on a wire rack to room temperature or serve warm.

Ricotta, Lemon and Basil Dip with Assorted Vegetables

Dips can be lean if they're made with low-calorie ingredients and if you use low-calorie raw or slightly steamed vegetables as dippers. Save this recipe for summer when fresh basil is in season or substitute fresh parsley. This tasty dip also works well as a spread on crostini.

The recipe is particularly nice for entertaining because it can be made ahead and refrigerated until serving time.

MAKES 1 CUP, 8 SERVINGS — 72 CALORIES PER SERVING

1 cup part-skim or reduced-fat ricotta cheese, liquid drained if necessary
1 tablespoon minced fresh basil or parsley
½ teaspoon grated lemon zest (yellow part only)
½ garlic clove, crushed through a press
¼ teaspoon salt
Freshly ground black pepper
1 tablespoon extra virgin olive oil
4 cups cut-up raw vegetables: carrot and celery sticks, strips of red, yellow and green bell peppers, cucumber slices and/or broccoli florets

1. In a medium bowl, combine the ricotta cheese, basil, lemon zest, garlic and salt. Stir until blended.

2. Scoop the dip into the center of a round serving dish. Grind black pepper over the top and drizzle with the olive oil. Arrange the raw vegetables around the dip. Serve cold.

Herb-Marinated Roasted Red Peppers

These savory peppers are high in flavor and low in calories. Serve them on their own, or use them as a condiment on sandwiches, in salads or as an accompaniment to simple grilled meats.

6 Servings | 37 Calories per serving

4 large red bell peppers
1 garlic clove, halved
1 teaspoon fresh oregano or 1/8 teaspoon dried
1/8 teaspoon salt
Freshly ground black pepper
1 tablespoon extra virgin olive oil

1. Preheat your broiler. Place a large sheet of aluminum foil in a 9 × 13-inch baking pan. Arrange the peppers on their sides in the baking pan. Broil as close as possible to the heat, turning the peppers, until they are evenly charred and blackened, about 10 minutes. Remove from the broiler and fold the foil over the peppers to enclose them; crimp the foil to seal. Let the peppers stand until cool enough to handle.

2. Working on a cutting board with a lip or groove to catch the juices, carefully peel the charred skin from the peppers. Cut the peppers in half and remove the seeds and stems. Remove any thick ribs from the peppers. Cut the roasted peppers into 1/4- to 1/2-inch-wide strips. Strain the juices left on the board through a sieve and reserve.

3. Rub a platter or shallow dish with the cut sides of the garlic; leave the garlic in the dish. Arrange the roasted pepper strips on the platter in an even layer. Drizzle the reserved pepper juice over the pepper strips. Season with the oregano, salt and a generous grinding of pepper. Drizzle the olive oil over the peppers.

4. Cover with plastic wrap and marinate 1 to 2 hours at room temperature or up to 2 days in the refrigerator. Serve at room temperature.

Variation

Simple Marinated Red Peppers: Drain 1 jar (12 ounces) roasted red peppers in a sieve and rinse under cold running water. Drain well and pat dry with a paper towel. Follow steps 3 and 4 in the recipe above, omitting the roasted pepper juices.

4 Servings — 54 Calories per serving

Black Olives Marinated with Lemon and Herbs

Use a swivel-bladed vegetable peeler to remove thin strips of the zest—the yellow part of the lemon. The flavor of this appetizer improves with age, so don't be tempted to rush the marinating time. Marinated olives will keep for up to two weeks in the refrigerator.

12 Servings — 85 Calories per serving

1 pound brine-cured black olives
4 strips of lemon zest (2 × ½ inch each), cut into long thin pieces
1 tablespoon fresh thyme sprigs
2 garlic cloves, bruised with side of a knife
⅛ teaspoon freshly ground black pepper
¼ cup extra virgin olive oil

1. In a container with a tight-fitting lid, combine the olives, lemon zest, fresh thyme sprigs, garlic, pepper and olive oil. Cover tightly and shake the container vigorously.

2. Marinate the olives in the refrigerator at least 2 days, stirring occasionally, before serving. Serve at room temperature.

Fresh Mozzarella Salad with Tomatoes and Basil

Fresh mozzarella cheese is now available in supermarkets across the country. It is marketed in three sizes: *ovoline* ("egg shaped"), *bocconcino* ("bite-size") or *ciliegine* ("little cherries"). Select whatever size you prefer, but cut the ovoline—the largest ball—into quarters for easier serving. The addition of crushed red pepper gives this salad a little extra zing.

6 Servings — 169 Calories per serving

2 tablespoons olive oil
2 garlic cloves, crushed through a press
½ teaspoon crushed hot red pepper
1 container (9 ounces) fresh mozzarella cheese—ciliegine or bocconcino, left whole; or (8 ounces) ovoline, quartered, drained and patted dry
⅛ teaspoon salt
1 pint basket cherry tomatoes, stems removed and halved if large
2 tablespoons torn fresh basil leaves or chopped Italian (flat leaf) parsley

1. In a small skillet, combine the olive oil, garlic and hot pepper. Cook gently over very low heat just until the garlic sizzles and the oil is warm, about 2 minutes; do not brown. Remove from the heat and let cool to room temperature.

2. Place the mozzarella cheese in a serving bowl and season with the salt. Drizzle the hot pepper and garlic-infused oil over the cheese. Toss to coat. Cover and marinate in the refrigerator 1 to 2 hours.

3. Let the salad stand at room temperature 20 minutes before serving. Just before serving, add the tomatoes and basil leaves and toss lightly.

Fresh Mozzarella and Bell Pepper Salad

6 Servings — 164 Calories per serving

½ garlic clove
1 package (9 ounces) smallest size fresh mozzarella cheese—ciliegine, packed in water, drained and patted dry (see Note)

½ medium red bell pepper, cut into ½-inch squares
½ medium green bell pepper, cut into ½-inch squares
2 tablespoons extra virgin olive oil
⅛ teaspoon salt
10 basil leaves or sprigs of Italian (flat leaf) parsley

1. Rub the inside of a medium bowl with the cut side of the garlic. Add the mozzarella cheese, red and green bell peppers, olive oil and salt. Toss to coat.

2. Just before serving, arrange the basil leaves on a small platter. Top with the mozzarella salad. Serve at room temperature.

NOTE *If ciliegine is not available, cut larger fresh mozzarella into ½-inch cubes.*

— *Fresh Mozzarella Salad with Roasted Peppers and Sun-Dried Tomatoes* —

Instead of fresh tomatoes, this salad uses strips of jarred roasted red peppers and the tantalizing taste of sun-dried tomatoes, which makes it perfect for winter occasions.

6 Servings — 165 Calories per serving

½ garlic clove
1 container (9 ounces) fresh mozzarella cheese—ciliegine or bocconcino, left whole; or (8 ounces) ovoline, quartered, drained and patted dry
¼ cup jarred roasted red peppers, rinsed, drained and cut into ¼-inch strips
1 tablespoon minced dry-packed Sonoma sun-dried tomatoes
2 tablespoons extra virgin olive oil
Pinch of dried oregano or thyme
Pinch of freshly ground black pepper

1. Rub the inside of a medium bowl with the cut side of the garlic. Add the mozzarella cheese, roasted red peppers, sun-dried tomatoes, olive oil, oregano and black pepper. Toss to coat.

2. Cover and marinate in the refrigerator 1 to 2 hours to allow the flavors to blend. Let stand at room temperature 20 minutes before serving.

Artichokes Vinaigrette

Artichokes are a dieter's delight. A medium globe artichoke contains less than 50 calories and virtually no fat or cholesterol. Here the artichokes are braised in savory broth before being lightly dressed with garlicky vinaigrette.

4 Servings — 85 Calories per serving

Juice of 1 lemon
2 large artichokes
1 leafy celery top
1 bay leaf
1 garlic clove, bruised with side of a knife
4 teaspoons olive oil
2 teaspoons red or white wine vinegar
½ garlic clove, crushed
⅛ teaspoon salt
Pinch of coarsely ground black pepper
1 tablespoon chopped fresh basil or parsley, for garnish

1. Squeeze the lemon juice into a large bowl half filled with water. Pull off and discard the small leaves at the base of the artichoke and the two bottom rows of larger leaves. Place each artichoke on its side and using a large stainless steel knife cut about ½ inch down from the top. Using a kitchen scissors, cut the hard tips off the remaining leaves. Cut the artichoke in half lengthwise. Pull out and discard the purple-tinged center leaves with the sharp tips. Using the tip of a teaspoon, scrape out and discard the fuzzy choke from the artichoke bottom. Submerge the artichoke in the lemon water.

2. In a large wide saucepan or skillet with a tight-fitting lid, combine 2 inches of water, the celery top, bay leaf and bruised garlic clove and bring to a boil. Drain the artichoke halves and add, cut sides down, to the skillet. Cover and cook over medium-low heat until the artichokes are tender when pierced with a fork, 15 to 20 minutes.

3. Lift the artichokes from the water, then arrange them, cut sides up, on a platter and let cool to room temperature. (The artichokes can be cooked ahead, covered and refrigerated for several hours until ready to serve.)

4. In a small bowl, whisk the oil, vinegar, crushed garlic, salt and pepper until blended. Spoon about 1 teaspoon of the vinaigrette over each artichoke half. Garnish with a sprinkling of chopped basil. Cover and marinate at room temperature at least 30 minutes before serving.

Marinated Artichoke Hearts

This simple, exceptionally light salad is especially attractive served on red radicchio leaves and garnished with black olives.

6 Servings — 78 Calories per serving

2 packages (9 ounces each) frozen artichoke hearts
2 tablespoons extra virgin olive oil
2 tablespoons fresh lemon juice
1 small red onion, cut into thin (¼-inch) wedges
½ lemon, halved again lengthwise, then cut into ¼-inch slices
1 tablespoon chopped fresh oregano or ¼ teaspoon dried
1 tablespoon coarsely chopped Italian (flat leaf) parsley
⅛ teaspoon salt
Pinch of freshly ground black pepper

1. Cook the frozen artichokes according to the package directions. Drain well and transfer the artichokes to a medium bowl. Let cool.

2. In a small bowl, whisk together the olive oil and lemon juice. Add to the artichokes along with the onion, lemon slices, oregano, parsley, salt and pepper. Toss to blend. Cover and marinate in the refrigerator several hours or overnight. Season with additional salt and pepper to taste before serving.

Baked Stuffed Artichokes

My mother served baked stuffed artichokes at every holiday dinner. Easily made ahead and then reheated, they are perfect for parties.

4 Servings　　169 Calories per serving

4 large artichokes
4 teaspoons olive oil
1 cup coarse dry bread crumbs (preferably made from day-old Italian bread)
1 garlic clove, crushed through a press
2 tablespoons grated Parmesan cheese
1/8 teaspoon freshly ground black pepper

1. Cut the stems from the artichokes so they sit evenly. Pull off the bottom row of leaves. Place each artichoke on its side and using a large stainless steel knife cut off about ½ inch down from the top. Using a kitchen scissors, cut the hard tips off of all the remaining leaves.

2. Stand the artichokes up in a large nonaluminum saucepan or Dutch oven wide enough to hold the artichokes tightly. Add enough water to come about halfway up the sides of the artichokes. Bring to a boil. Cover and cook over medium-low heat until the artichokes are tender, about 40 to 50 minutes. Lift the artichokes from the saucepan and invert on a folded kitchen towel to drain; let cool to room temperature.

3. Spread the leaves apart and pull out and discard the sharp-tipped purplish leaves. With the tip of a teaspoon, scrap out the fuzzy choke in the center of each artichoke.

4. Preheat the oven to 400° F. Place the artichokes in a baking dish. Heat the olive oil in a medium skillet. Add the bread crumbs and cook over medium-low heat, stirring, until they are lightly toasted and golden, about 10 minutes. Add the garlic and cook 1 minute longer. Remove from the heat. Stir in 1 tablespoon of the Parmesan cheese and the pepper.

5. Spread the leaves of the artichokes apart and sprinkle about ¼ cup of the seasoned bread crumbs into each artichoke, tucking the mixture loosely between the leaves.

6. Sprinkle the remaining 1 tablespoon cheese over the artichokes. Bake until the bread crumbs are crisp and golden, 15 to 20 minutes. Serve the stuffed artichokes warm or at room temperature.

— *Baked Tomatoes with Garlic Crumb Topping* —

Tomatoes, which have no fat and very few calories, are topped here with a simple but savory bread crumb, herb and olive oil topping and baked until golden and fragrant. They make a marvelous addition to an antipasto plate, or they can be served as a vegetable accompaniment, especially appropriate with grilled chicken or roast lamb.

8 Servings — 64 Calories per serving

1 garlic clove, halved
8 small ripe tomatoes
1/8 teaspoon salt
Pinch of freshly ground black pepper
1 tablespoon finely chopped fresh basil or parsley
2 tablespoons olive oil
1 cup coarse dry bread crumbs (preferably made from day-old Italian bread)
1 teaspoon chopped fresh oregano or a pinch of dried
1 teaspoon fresh thyme or a pinch of dried

1. Preheat the oven to 375° F. Rub a shallow 9 × 13-inch baking dish with the cut sides of the garlic; reserve the garlic for the crumbs.

2. Cut ½ inch from the tops of the tomatoes. Arrange the tomatoes in a single layer, cut sides up, in the baking dish. Season lightly with the salt and pepper; top with the basil leaves, dividing evenly. Drizzle 1 tablespoon of the olive oil over the tomatoes.

3. Crush half of the reserved garlic in a garlic press; toss with the bread crumbs, oregano, thyme and remaining 1 tablespoon olive oil. Sprinkle the crumbs over the tomatoes. Bake until the crumbs are lightly browned, 15 to 20 minutes. Serve warm or at room temperature.

– *Roasted Zucchini and Red Onion Vinaigrette* –

4 Servings 71 Calories per serving

4 teaspoons olive oil
1 large red onion, cut into 1/4-inch slices
1 strip of orange zest (2 × 1/2 inch)
1 teaspoon fresh thyme or 1/4 teaspoon dried
4 small zucchini (about 4 inches long), halved lengthwise
1 tablespoon red wine vinegar
1/4 teaspoon salt
1/8 teaspoon freshly ground black pepper

1. Preheat the oven to 400° F. Combine the olive oil, red onion, orange zest and thyme in a 9 × 13-inch baking dish. Stir to blend. Bake, stirring once or twice, until the onion begins to brown, about 15 minutes.

2. Add the zucchini, cut sides down, and spoon the onion mixture over the vegetable. Bake until the zucchini are tender, about 10 minutes. Remove from the oven and let cool slightly.

3. Arrange on a serving plate and sprinkle evenly with the vinegar, salt and pepper. Toss gently. Serve at room temperature.

Baked Stuffed Mushroom Caps

Isn't it nice to know that you don't have to give up some of your favorite appetizers, even if you're eating a lighter diet. Mushrooms, which contain no fat or cholesterol, are also exceptionally low in calories. Look for extra-large mushrooms, sometimes called stuffing mushrooms, for this very simple, delicious appetizer.

4 Servings 62 Calories per serving

9 large mushrooms (about 1/2 pound)
1 tablespoon olive oil
1/4 cup finely chopped onion
1/3 cup coarse dry bread crumbs (preferably made from day-old Italian bread)

1 small garlic clove, crushed through a press
1/2 teaspoon minced fresh oregano or thyme or 1/8 teaspoon dried
1/8 teaspoon salt
Freshly ground black pepper
1 tablespoon grated Parmesan cheese

1. Wipe the mushrooms clean with a damp paper towel. Remove the stems and reserve them. Brush 8 of the mushroom caps lightly with 1 teaspoon of the olive oil. Arrange the 8 mushroom caps, stem sides up, in a baking dish. Add 2 tablespoons of water to the dish. Finely chop the reserved stems and the remaining mushroom; there will be about 1 cup chopped mushrooms; set aside.

2. Preheat the oven to 400° F. In a large nonstick skillet, heat the remaining 2 teaspoons olive oil. Add the chopped mushrooms and the onion and cook over medium-high heat, stirring, until lightly browned, about 5 minutes. Add the bread crumbs, garlic, oregano, salt and pepper. Reduce the heat to medium and cook, stirring, until the bread is lightly toasted, 3 to 5 minutes. Stir in the Parmesan cheese.

3. Stuff the mushroom caps with the bread crumb and mushroom mixture, pressing lightly with the back of a spoon. Bake, uncovered, until the stuffing is well browned and the mushroom caps are tender, about 25 minutes. Serve hot or at room temperature.

Variation

Baked Sausage-Stuffed Mushroom Caps: Cut the fat and calories in this recipe even more by using Italian-style turkey sausage instead of pork sausage.

In a medium skillet, cook 2 links (about 3 ounces) Italian sausage, removed from the casings, in a medium saucepan until well browned; drain off all the fat. Make Baked Stuffed Mushroom Caps as described above, but at the end of step 2 combine the cooked sausage with the cooked mushrooms and onion mixture, bread crumbs and seasonings.

4 Servings — 112 Calories per serving

— *Baked Mushrooms with Garlic Bread Crumbs* —

4 Servings — 70 Calories per serving

12 large mushrooms
1 tablespoon olive oil
½ cup coarse dry bread crumbs (preferably made from day-old Italian bread)
1 garlic clove, crushed through a press
½ teaspoon fresh thyme or ¼ teaspoon dried
⅛ teaspoon salt
⅛ teaspoon freshly ground black pepper

1. Preheat the oven to 400° F. Wipe the mushrooms clean with a damp paper towel. Cut lengthwise through the stems into ¼-inch-thick slices. Lightly brush a 7 × 9-inch baking dish with 1 teaspoon of the olive oil.

2. Heat the remaining 2 teaspoons oil in a medium skillet. Add the bread crumbs and cook over medium heat, stirring, until the crumbs are coated with oil and begin to brown, about 5 minutes. Stir in the garlic, thyme, salt and pepper. Cook, stirring, until the garlic is fragrant and slightly softened, 1 to 2 minutes.

3. Sprinkle the crumb mixture evenly over the mushrooms. Bake 25 minutes, or until the mushrooms are tender. Serve hot or at room temperature.

Marinated Mushrooms

The longer these mushrooms are marinated the better the flavor. Serve with toothpicks as an hors d'oeuvre, or toss as an extra fillip into a mixed green salad.

8 Servings — 61 Calories per serving

10 ounces large white button mushrooms
¼ cup white wine vinegar
¼ cup fresh lemon juice
3 tablespoons olive oil
2 tablespoons orange juice
1 celery rib with leafy top—leafy top chopped, rib thinly sliced
1 garlic clove, crushed through a press

1 teaspoon fresh thyme or ¼ teaspoon dried
½ teaspoon grated orange zest
¼ teaspoon salt
⅛ teaspoon freshly ground black pepper
½ medium red onion, thinly sliced

1. Wipe the mushrooms clean with a damp paper towel. Cut them lengthwise into ¼-inch-thick slices.

2. In a medium bowl, whisk together the vinegar, lemon juice, olive oil, orange juice, chopped celery top, garlic, thyme, orange zest, salt and pepper until blended. Add the mushrooms, red onion and sliced celery rib; toss to coat.

3. Cover and refrigerate at least 2 hours or overnight, stirring once or twice. Before serving, let stand at room temperature 30 minutes.

Grilled Zucchini with Mint

This recipe is best when your garden—or local farmer's market—is loaded with zucchini, which should not be more than 4 inches in length.

4 Servings — 68 Calories per serving

1 tablespoon olive oil
1 small garlic clove, crushed through a press
8 small zucchini, halved lengthwise
2 tablespoons finely chopped fresh mint or 2 teaspoons dried, crumbled
2 tablespoons cider vinegar
1 teaspoon sugar

1. Place the olive oil and garlic on a platter. Add the zucchini and turn to coat the cut sides with the oil and garlic.

2. Preheat your broiler or light a hot fire in a grill. Arrange the zucchini on the broiler pan, cut sides up, or on the hot grill, cut sides down. (Set the platter aside for later; do not rinse.) Cook, moving the zucchini so that they cook evenly, until the cut sides are golden, about 5 minutes; the exact time will depend on the intensity of the heat. Turn and cook until tender, 1 to 2 minutes longer. Remove from the heat.

3. Meanwhile, add the mint, vinegar and sugar to the platter with the garlic oil on it. Stir with a fork to blend. Add the zucchini, a few at a time, turning to coat with the vinegar and mint. Serve at room temperature.

Baked Stuffed Baby Eggplant

These pretty eggplant boats are stuffed with a savory filling flecked with pieces of sautéed red bell pepper. If the dark purple baby Italian eggplant, which are only 4 or 5 inches long, are not available in your market, use the smallest regular eggplants you can find and cut each half lengthwise in half just before serving.

4 Servings | 91 Calories per serving

4 baby eggplant or 2 small eggplant (about 1 pound total)
4 teaspoons olive oil
½ cup chopped onion
½ cup chopped red bell pepper
1 garlic clove, crushed through a press
½ cup coarse dry bread crumbs (preferably made from day-old Italian bread)
1 tablespoon chopped fresh parsley
½ teaspoon minced fresh oregano or ⅛ teaspoon dried
¼ teaspoon salt
⅛ teaspoon freshly ground black pepper

1. Preheat the oven to 400° F. Halve the eggplant lengthwise. Brush the cut sides lightly with 2 teaspoons of the olive oil. Place, cut sides down, in a large baking dish. Bake 15 minutes, or until tender. Remove from the oven and let stand until cool enough to handle. With a spoon, scoop out the cooked eggplant to leave a thin shell, being careful not to tear the skin. Coarsely chop the eggplant. Reserve the shells.

2. Heat the remaining 2 teaspoons olive oil in a large nonstick skillet. Add the onion and red pepper and cook over medium-low heat, stirring occasionally, until the onion, is golden, about 10 minutes. Add the chopped eggplant to the skillet along with the garlic. Cook, stirring often, until the eggplant is very soft, about 5 minutes. Add the bread crumbs, parsley, oregano, salt and pepper. Cook, stirring, until heated through, about 1 minute.

3. Carefully spoon the eggplant-bread crumb filling into the scooped out shells, dividing evenly. Bake 15 minutes, or until heated through. Serve warm or at room temperature.

Herb-Marinated Baked Eggplant Slices

Baking provides a no-fuss, efficient way for cooking eggplant that requires very little oil.

6 SERVINGS 79 CALORIES PER SERVING

1 medium eggplant (1 to 1¼ pounds), peeled and cut into 12 slices ¼ inch thick
Salt
3 tablespoons olive oil
1 garlic clove, crushed through a press
½ teaspoon fresh rosemary or ½ teaspoon dried
½ teaspoon fresh thyme or ¼ teaspoon dried
½ teaspoon fresh oregano or ¼ teaspoon dried
Freshly ground black pepper
1½ tablespoons red wine vinegar

1. Sprinkle the eggplant lightly with salt and layer in a colander set in the sink. Weight down with a plate and let stand 1 to 2 hours. Rinse the eggplant slices well and pat dry with paper towels.

2. Preheat the oven to 425° F. Combine 2 tablespoons of the olive oil and the garlic in a small bowl. Lightly brush both sides of the eggplant slices with the garlic oil. Arrange the eggplant in a single layer on a baking sheet. Combine the rosemary, thyme, oregano and ¼ teaspoon salt in a small bowl; sprinkle the top of each eggplant slice evenly with the herbs. Add a grinding of black pepper.

3. Bake the eggplant, turning once, until browned and tender, about 10 minutes per side. Whisk the remaining 1 tablespoon olive oil and the red wine vinegar until blended; sprinkle over the eggplant. Serve warm or at room temperature.

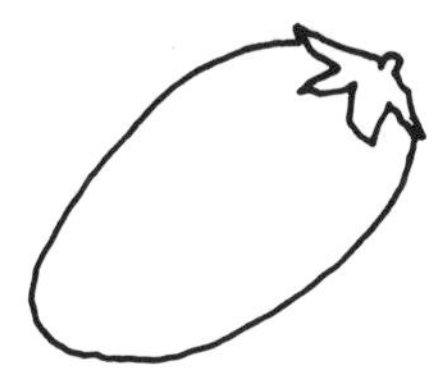

Baked Rolled Stuffed Eggplant

Here slices of eggplant are stuffed with an herbed cheese filling, rolled up and topped with a light tomato and eggplant sauce. For convenience at a dinner party, the dish can be completely assembled several hours ahead and baked at the last moment. This recipe makes a nice hot antipasto, and because it is so light and delicious—and well under 100 calories a portion—you might want to double the servings and enjoy it as a main course.

5 Servings — 88 Calories per serving

1 large eggplant (1½ pounds), peeled
Salt
1 tablespoon olive oil
2 tablespoons finely chopped onion
½ garlic clove, crushed through a press
1 can (14 ounces) Italian-style plum tomatoes, with their juices
2 tablespoons chopped fresh basil or parsley
¼ teaspoon salt
⅛ teaspoon freshly ground black pepper
½ cup nonfat ricotta cheese
1 tablespoon grated Parmesan cheese

1. Cut the eggplant lengthwise into 7 slices, each about ½ inch thick. Finely chop the 2 rounded end slices and set aside. Sprinkle the remaining eggplant slices lightly with salt. Layer in a colander set in the sink. Weight down with a plate and let stand 1 to 2 hours. Rinse the eggplant slices well and pat dry with paper towels.

2. Preheat the oven to 400° F. Lightly brush both sides of the eggplant slices with 2 teaspoons of the olive oil. Arrange the eggplant in a single layer on a baking sheet and bake until the bottoms are lightly browned, about 15 minutes. Remove from the oven.

3. Meanwhile, heat the remaining 1 teaspoon oil in a large nonstick skillet. Add the onion and cook over medium-low heat, stirring occasionally, until tender, about 5 minutes. Stir in the reserved chopped eggplant, cover and reduce the heat to low. Cook 10 minutes, or until the eggplant is tender. Stir in the garlic until blended. Add the tomatoes with their juices. Bring to a boil, breaking up the tomatoes with the side of a fork. Reduce the heat to medium-low and simmer, stirring, until the sauce is thickened, about 15 minutes. Season with 1 tablespoon of the basil, the salt and pepper. Remove from the heat.

4. In a small bowl, combine the ricotta cheese, Parmesan cheese and the remaining basil. Stir until blended. Spread about 1 tablespoon of the tomato sauce over each eggplant slice. Spoon 2 tablespoons of the ricotta cheese mixture crosswise across the middle of each slice. Bring up the two ends of the eggplant to overlap, enclosing the filling and forming a loose roll.

5. Spoon the remaining tomato sauce into a shallow 1½-quart baking dish. Arrange the stuffed eggplant rolls, seam sides down, on top of the sauce. Cover with aluminum foil and bake 15 minutes, or until heated through.

Baked Tomatoes Stuffed with Rice

4 Servings | 195 Calories per serving

4 teaspoons olive oil
4 medium tomatoes
⅛ teaspoon salt
Freshly ground black pepper
½ cup diced red onion
½ cup cooked fresh or thawed frozen tiny green peas
1½ cups cooked rice
2 tablespoons chopped fresh basil or Italian (flat leaf) parsley
4 teaspoons grated Parmesan cheese

1. Preheat the oven to 400° F. Coat the bottom of a 9-inch square baking dish with ½ teaspoon of the olive oil.

2. Cut the tops from the tomatoes. Squeeze the juice into a strainer set over a small bowl; reserve the juice. Scoop out the pulp from the inside of the tomatoes. Chop the pulp and reserve. Arrange the tomatoes in the baking dish. Rub ¼ teaspoon of the olive oil on the outside of each tomato. Season the inside of the tomatoes with the salt and a grinding of pepper.

3. Heat the remaining 2½ teaspoons olive oil in a medium nonstick skillet. Add the onion and cook over moderate heat, stirring, until softened, about 3 minutes. Add the peas and cook 2 minutes. Add the rice, the reserved tomato pulp and juices and the basil. Cook, stirring, just to blend and heat through, about 1 minute. Carefully spoon into each tomato, dividing evenly and pressing down lightly with the back of a spoon.

4. Sprinkle 1 teaspoon of the Parmesan cheese over the top of each tomato. Bake 20 to 25 minutes, until the tomatoes are tender and the cheese is lightly browned. Serve warm or at room temperature.

Caponata

Serve this zesty spread on crackers or crostini.

8 Servings | 57 Calories per serving

1 large eggplant (1¼ to 1½ pounds)
2 tablespoons olive oil
½ cup diced red onion
½ cup diced celery
1 garlic clove, minced
1 cup diced plum tomatoes (about 3 tomatoes)
2 tablespoons chopped Italian (flat leaf) parsley
1 tablespoon red wine vinegar
1 tablespoon finely chopped pitted green olives
1 teaspoon capers, rinsed and drained
¼ teaspoon salt
⅛ teaspoon freshly ground black pepper

1. Preheat the oven to 350° F. Trim the eggplant and cut in half lengthwise. Place the eggplant, cut sides down, in a baking pan. Bake until the eggplant is soft and beginning to collapse, about 45 minutes. Remove from the oven and let stand until cool enough to handle. With a spoon, scoop out the cooked eggplant and cut into ½-inch dice. Discard the skin.

2. In a large nonstick skillet, heat the olive oil. Add the onion, celery and garlic and cook over medium-low heat, stirring occasionally, until tender, about 5 minutes.

3. Add the diced eggplant to the skillet. Increase the heat to medium and cook, stirring often, until the eggplant begins to brown, about 10 minutes. Add the tomatoes and parsley. Reduce the heat to low and cook, uncovered, stirring occasionally, 10 minutes. Add the red wine vinegar, olives and capers. Season with the salt and pepper.

4. Let the caponata cool to room temperature. The recipe can be made up to 2 days ahead. Refrigerate, tightly covered; let return to room temperature before serving.

Polenta Toasts with Red Pepper Purée

The recipe for roasting and peeling red bell peppers is on p. 24, but, if preferred, you can use jarred roasted red peppers. A 12-ounce jar is equal to about 2 whole roasted and peeled red bell peppers.

4 Servings — 159 Calories per serving

2 teaspoons olive oil
2 tablespoons finely chopped onion
1 garlic clove, crushed through a press
1 teaspoon chopped fresh oregano or a pinch of dried
2 large red bell peppers, roasted and peeled, or 1 jar (12 ounces), rinsed, drained and coarsely cut up
2 tablespoons unsalted or reduced-sodium chicken broth
1/8 teaspoon salt
1/8 teaspoon freshly ground black pepper
12 Polenta Toasts (p. 42)

1. Heat the olive oil in a small nonstick skillet. Add the onion and cook over medium-low heat, stirring often, until golden, about 5 minutes. Add the garlic and oregano and cook 30 seconds longer.

2. Stir in the red peppers; stir just to blend. Transfer to a food processor, add the chicken broth and purée until smooth. Transfer to a serving bowl and season with the salt and pepper.

3. Spread about 3/4 tablespoon of the red pepper purée over each polenta triangle. Serve warm or at room temperature.

Sautéed Mushrooms on Polenta Toasts

When they are available, substitute cultivated exotic mushrooms such as *shiitake* or *pleurotes* (oyster mushrooms) for part of the white button mushrooms.

4 Servings | 179 Calories per serving

1 tablespoon olive oil
10 ounces white button mushrooms, thinly sliced
½ cup sliced red onion
1 garlic clove, crushed through a press
1 tablespoon chopped fresh parsley
1 teaspoon minced fresh oregano or ¼ teaspoon dried
¼ teaspoon salt
⅛ teaspoon freshly ground black pepper
16 Polenta Toasts (recipe follows)

1. Heat the olive oil in a large nonstick skillet. Add the mushrooms and red onion. Cook over medium heat, stirring occasionally, until the mushrooms are golden, about 10 minutes. Add the garlic, parsley and oregano. Cook 1 minute longer.

2. Season the mushrooms with the salt and pepper. Spoon the mixture over the Polenta Toasts, dividing it evenly.

Polenta Toasts

Polenta, a creamy mixture of cornmeal and broth flavored with Parmesan cheese and sautéed onion, is traditionally served with *ossobuco* (a stew of veal shanks). It is also good with rabbit, chicken or other meats cooked in a stewlike mixture. Here polenta is spread in a baking dish to cool and then cut into triangles, which are browned in the oven or in a skillet. The triangles are delicious served here as an antipasto, topped with sautéed mushrooms or puréed marinated red bell peppers; or they can be offered as a side dish with grilled meats or poultry.

4 Servings | 123 Calories per serving

1 tablespoon olive oil
2 tablespoons finely chopped onion
1 garlic clove, crushed through a press
1½ cups unsalted or reduced-sodium chicken broth, or ¾ cup broth and ¾ cup water
½ cup yellow cornmeal
½ cup skim milk
1 tablespoon grated Parmesan cheese
¼ teaspoon salt
⅛ teaspoon freshly ground black pepper
Vegetable cooking spray

1. Heat 2 teaspoons of the olive oil in a medium saucepan. Add the onion and cook over low heat, stirring occasionally, until tender, about 5 minutes. Add the garlic and cook 30 seconds longer.

2. Combine the broth and the cornmeal in a bowl; stir until smooth. Add the cornmeal paste to the onion in the saucepan. Stir in the milk. Stir over medium heat until the mixture begins to boil. Reduce the heat to medium-low and cook, stirring and adjusting the heat if necessary so that the mixture does not sputter excessively, until the polenta is smooth and very thick, about 10 minutes. Stir in the Parmesan cheese, salt and pepper.

3. Spray a 9-inch square baking dish with vegetable cooking spray. Add the polenta and smooth the top with a rubber spatula. Cover with plastic wrap and refrigerate until cooled and set, at least 1 hour. Cut the polenta into 9 squares; cut each square diagonally into 2 triangles.

4. Heat the remaining 1 teaspoon olive oil in a large nonstick skillet over medium-low heat. Add the polenta triangles and cook until well browned and crisp on one side, about 3 minutes. Turn and cook until browned on the other side, about 3 minutes longer. Repeat until all the triangles are browned. To oven-brown, preheat the oven to 400° F. Brush a large nonstick baking sheet with a thin film of olive oil. Arrange the polenta triangles on the baking sheet. Bake, turning once, until browned, about 10 minutes.

Chapter Two

SOUPS

There are probably as many "Italian" soups as there are Italian cooks. Because they tend not to include milk, cream, butter and other high-fat ingredients, the soups are naturally healthful and low in calories. Most of the tempting combinations of simmering broth, vegetables, beans, legumes, rice and pasta in this chapter rely on only a tablespoon or less of olive oil for sautéing vegetables or to add a little extra flavor, which is how I've managed to keep all the calorie counts in these recipes down to 200 or less per serving.

While the portions listed in the following recipes are designed to serve as first-course offerings, many of the heartier soups could easily constitute a dinner in a bowl. The bean soups in particular—Minestrone, Cannellini Bean, Ham and Escarole Soup, White Bean Soup with Orange Gremolata, Chick Pea and Tomato Soup, and Lentil, Rice and Mushroom Soup—are all substantial enough to make a meal in themselves. If you wish to embellish the menu, a tossed salad or a basket of crusty Italian bread and a chunk of cheese would more than suffice.

These thick, legume-based soups, which, except for the broth, are either strictly vegetarian or include just a small amount of meat for flavor, are exceptionally typical of home-style Italian cooking at its best. Everybody's Italian mother, grandmother or aunt has her own recipes for *pasta e fagioli,* Pasta and Bean Soup, which probably evokes fond memories from childhood. While both pasta and beans in the same dish may sound a little unusual to an American palate, don't dismiss the combination until you try it. It's addicting.

Some of the lighter soups—Tomato and Two-Mushroom Soup or

Creamy Spinach Soup—can be combined with small portions of pizza or other main dish selections to round out a healthy and satisfying menu.

While homemade unsalted chicken stock is, of course, first choice as a base for many of these soups, a good brand of reduced-sodium chicken broth is a convenient substitute. It allows the kind of last-minute, pull-it-together-from-scratch supper that is the hallmark of a good cook.

Cannellini Bean, Ham and Escarole Soup

Beans are low in fat and they have no cholesterol, but they are packed with carbohydrates, which add up to calories. It's nice to know even calorie counters can enjoy the healthy legumes, as long as they are combined with vegetables and other lean ingredients. This soup is substantial enough to serve for supper, with a slice of pizza or garlic toast and a salad on the side.

6 Servings — 198 Calories per serving

1 tablespoon olive oil
½ cup chopped onion
1 garlic clove, crushed through a press
2 cans (19 ounces each) cannellini (white kidney beans), liquid reserved
4 cups unsalted or reduced-sodium chicken broth
1 carrot, peeled and thinly sliced
¼ cup slivered baked ham (about 2 ounces)
1 bay leaf
2 cups packed coarsely chopped fresh escarole, kale or spinach
Salt and freshly ground black pepper

1. Heat the olive oil in a large heavy saucepan. Add the onion and cook over low heat, stirring occasionally, until tender, about 5 minutes. Add the garlic and cook 1 minute longer.

2. Add the beans with their liquid, the chicken broth, carrot, ham, bay leaf and 2 cups water. Bring to a boil, stirring occasionally. Cover and simmer over low heat 10 minutes.

3. Add the greens and cook, covered, until tender, about 12 minutes for escarole or kale, 3 to 5 minutes for spinach. Because the beans are salty, taste the soup before seasoning with salt and pepper.

Minestrone

There are as many versions of minestrone as there are cooks who make it. Two necessary ingredients for this rich, thick soup are a well-flavored beef broth and the very freshest vegetables you can find. Note that despite the fact that it's chock-full of vegetables and flavored with prosciutto and Parmesan cheese, this soup still comes in at under 150 calories a bowl.

8 Servings — 136 Calories per serving

1 tablespoon olive oil
1 tablespoon diced prosciutto, pancetta or smoked ham
1 medium carrot, peeled and sliced
1 medium onion, diced
1 celery rib, chopped
1 garlic clove, minced
2 tablespoons minced Italian (flat leaf) parsley
6 cups beef broth, preferably unsalted, well skimmed
1 cup diced red potatoes
½ cup diced peeled parsnip (optional)
2 cups packed torn Swiss chard or escarole
1 cup thinly shredded Savoy cabbage
1 cup canned cannellini (white kidney beans), rinsed and drained
1 cup peeled diced fresh tomatoes or drained and diced canned Italian-style plum tomatoes
½ cup ditalini, tubettini or tubetti pasta
½ cup diced zucchini
½ cup fresh or thawed frozen green peas
½ cup cut (½ inch) fresh green beans
½ teaspoon salt
⅛ teaspoon freshly ground black pepper
3 tablespoons grated Parmesan cheese

1. Heat the olive oil in a large heavy saucepan or Dutch oven. Add the prosciutto and cook over medium-low heat, stirring occasionally, 5 minutes. Add the carrot, onion, celery, garlic and parsley and cook 5 minutes. Cover, reduce the heat to low and cook 10 minutes.

2. Stir in the beef broth and bring to a boil. Add the potatoes and parsnip. Cover and simmer 20 minutes. Stir in the Swiss chard, cabbage, cannellini and tomatoes. Simmer, partially covered, 30 minutes.

3. Stir the pasta, zucchini, peas and green beans into the soup. Simmer, uncovered, stirring occasionally, until the pasta is tender, about 15 minutes. Season with the salt and pepper. Ladle into bowls and sprinkle each serving with about 1 teaspoon Parmesan cheese.

Broccoli and Orzo Soup

Orzo, a tiny rice-shaped pasta, and broccoli cook quickly in broth to create a light, nourishing soup that can be prepared in about 20 minutes. Substitute rice or other small pasta shapes, such as pastina, stelline or even alphabets, for the orzo, if you like.

5 Servings | 176 Calories per serving

8 cups unsalted or reduced-sodium chicken broth
4 cups chopped fresh broccoli, including peeled stems
1 carrot, peeled and diced
½ cup orzo or other tiny pasta
½ cup chopped drained peeled and seeded canned tomatoes
¼ cup grated Parmesan cheese
Freshly ground black pepper

1. In a large saucepan, bring the chicken broth to a boil. Add the broccoli, carrot and orzo. Cook over medium heat, stirring occasionally, until the pasta and vegetables are tender, about 15 minutes.

2. Add the tomatoes and Parmesan cheese and simmer 5 minutes longer. Ladle into soup bowls and top with a grinding of pepper.

— *White Bean Soup with Orange Gremolata* —

Traditionally, *gremolata* is a finely chopped mixture of parsley, lemon peel and raw garlic. Added at the end of the cooking time, it adds a fresh, light flavor to rich dishes, such as *ossobuco.* Here, orange is used instead of lemon. The striking flavor and satisfaction of the beans will make you marvel at the low calorie count of this delicious soup.

8 Servings — 176 Calories per serving

¾ pound dried small white or Great Northern beans, rinsed and picked over to remove any grit
1 tablespoon olive oil
1 cup diced onion
1 cup diced trimmed celery with leafy tops
1 cup diced peeled carrot
1 bay leaf
½ teaspoon salt
Freshly ground black pepper
⅓ cup packed cut-up Italian (flat leaf) parsley sprigs
2 garlic cloves, chopped
1 strip of orange zest (2 × ½ inch), chopped

1. In a large saucepan or Dutch oven, soak the beans in water to cover overnight. Or combine the beans and water in a large pot, bring to a boil and boil, uncovered, 2 minutes; cover and let stand 1 hour. Drain well.

2. In the same large saucepan or Dutch oven, heat the olive oil. Add the onion, celery and carrot and cook 1 minute, stirring, just to coat with oil. Cover and cook over low heat, stirring occasionally, until tender, about 15 minutes; do not let brown.

3. Add the drained soaked beans, 12 cups (3 quarts) of fresh cold water and the bay leaf. Bring to a boil, reduce the heat to low and cook, uncovered, 2 to 2½ hours, or until the beans are very tender and the liquid is reduced by one third.

4. Let the soup cool slightly. Ladle out about 2 cups of the cooked beans with some of the liquid and purée in a food processor or blender. Stir the purée back into the soup. Season with the salt and a generous grinding of pepper.

5. Just before serving, finely chop the parsley, garlic and orange zest in a food processor or by hand to make the gremolata. Ladle the simmering soup into bowls and stir about 1 teaspoonful of the gremolata into each serving.

Chick Pea and Tomato Soup

Canned chick peas, also known as garbanzo beans or *ceci* in Italian, are convenient and nutritious in this hearty soup. At the height of tomato season use peeled fresh tomatoes; otherwise good-quality canned Italian-style plum tomatoes will serve well.

4 Servings 178 Calories per serving

1 tablespoon olive oil
½ cup chopped onion
½ cup sliced celery
1 garlic clove, crushed through a press
3½ cups peeled, cored and coarsely chopped tomatoes, with their juices, or 1 can (28 ounces) Italian-style plum tomatoes, coarsely chopped, juices reserved
2 cups unsalted or reduced-sodium chicken broth
1 bay leaf
½ teaspoon dried sage
1 can (19 ounces) chick peas, rinsed and drained
2 tablespoons finely chopped Italian (flat leaf) parsley
⅛ teaspoon salt
Freshly ground black pepper

1. Heat the olive oil in a large wide saucepan or Dutch oven. Add the onion and celery and cook over low heat, stirring occasionally, until tender, about 8 minutes. Add the garlic and cook 2 minutes longer.

2. Add the tomatoes with their juices, the chicken broth, bay leaf and sage. Bring to a boil over high heat. Reduce the heat to low and cook, covered, 20 minutes.

3. Add the chick peas, parsley, salt and a generous grinding of pepper. Bring to a boil. Ladle into soup bowls and serve.

Pasta and Bean Soup

Pasta e fagioli, or pasta and beans, is a staple main dish soup in many Italian kitchens. Portion control and low fat is the key to enjoying such a hearty soup and still eating lean.

6 SERVINGS | 199 CALORIES PER SERVING

1 cup (about ½ pound) dried cannellini, or other white bean, rinsed and picked over to remove any grit
1 tablespoon olive oil
1 thin slice of prosciutto, pancetta or smoked ham, finely diced (about 1 tablespoon)
½ cup chopped onion
½ cup sliced celery
½ cup diced (¼ inch) peeled carrot
2 garlic cloves, minced
1 can (14 ounces) Italian-style plum tomatoes, with their juices
1 bay leaf
½ cup small shells, elbows or ditalini
½ teaspoon salt
3 tablespoons grated Parmesan cheese

1. In a large saucepan or Dutch oven, soak the beans in water to cover overnight. Or combine the beans and water in a large pot, bring to a boil and boil, uncovered, 1 minute; remove the saucepan from the heat, cover and let stand 1 hour. Drain well.

2. Heat the olive oil in a large wide saucepan or the Dutch oven. Add the prosciutto, onion, celery and carrot and cook over low heat, stirring occasionally, until tender, about 10 minutes. Add the garlic and cook 1 minute longer.

3. Add the drained soaked beans, 8 cups (2 quarts) of water, the tomatoes with their juices and the bay leaf. Bring to a boil, reduce the heat to low and cook, uncovered, until the beans are very tender and the soup is thickened, about 2 hours.

4. Stir in the pasta and salt. Simmer, stirring often, until the pasta is tender, about 15 minutes. Stir 1½ tablespoons of the Parmesan cheese into the soup. Ladle into bowls and sprinkle ¾ teaspoon of the remaining Parmesan cheese over each serving.

Lentil, Rice and Mushroom Soup

The advantage of using lentils instead of dried beans is that lentils don't require soaking, and they cook in less than 30 minutes.

8 Servings — 200 Calories per serving

1½ cups (about ¾ pound) lentils, rinsed and picked over to remove any grit
5 cups unsalted or reduced-sodium chicken broth and 5 cups water, or 10 cups water
1 bay leaf
½ cinnamon stick (about 1 inch long)
2 teaspoons olive oil
½ pound white button mushrooms, thinly sliced (about 2 cups)
1 cup chopped onion
½ cup diced (¼ inch) peeled carrot
⅓ cup long-grain white rice
1 garlic clove, crushed through a press
2 cups packed fresh spinach (optional)
½ teaspoon salt
⅛ teaspoon freshly ground black pepper

1. Combine the lentils, broth and water, bay leaf and cinnamon stick in a large saucepan or Dutch oven. Bring to a boil, reduce the heat to medium-low and cook, uncovered, until the lentils are tender, 20 to 30 minutes.

2. Meanwhile, heat the olive oil in a large skillet. Add the mushrooms, onion and carrot and cook over medium heat, stirring occasionally, until the vegetables are tender and the mushrooms begin to brown, about 10 minutes. Add the rice and garlic and stir to coat with the oil.

3. Add the mushroom-rice mixture to the cooked lentils. Add the spinach. Cook over medium-low heat, stirring occasionally, until the rice is tender, about 20 minutes. Add additional water or broth to thin the soup if it becomes too thick. Season with the salt and pepper.

Creamy Spinach Soup

This pretty green soup gets its creamy texture from a purée of fresh spinach and potatoes that have been cooked together in broth. There is no butter or cream added.

4 Servings — 199 Calories per serving

2 teaspoons olive oil
1 cup chopped onion
1 garlic clove, minced
4 cups packed fresh spinach (about 1½ pounds)
1 pound potatoes, peeled and cut into ½-inch dice
6 cups unsalted or reduced-sodium chicken broth
¼ teaspoon salt
2 tablespoons grated Parmesan cheese

1. Heat the olive oil in a large nonaluminum saucepan, preferably nonstick, or in a Dutch oven. Add the onion and cook over low heat, stirring occasionally, until tender, about 10 minutes. Add the garlic and cook 1 minute longer.

2. Add the spinach and potatoes. Cook, stirring, until the spinach is wilted and the vegetables are coated with the oil, about 5 minutes.

3. Add the chicken broth and salt and heat to simmering. Reduce the heat to low, cover and cook 30 minutes. Remove the cover and cook 30 minutes. Remove the pan from the heat and let the soup cool slightly.

4. Purée the soup in batches in a food processor or blender. Return the puréed soup to the saucepan and reheat. Stir in the Parmesan cheese and ladle into bowls.

Tomato and Two-Mushroom Soup

Both dried and fresh mushrooms contribute to the complex taste of this intriguing soup. Dried porcini, usually sold in small cellophane packages in Italian stores, specialty food shops and some supermarkets, have a robust aroma and flavor. Cremini mushrooms are similar in appearance to the more familiar fresh white button mushrooms, except that the cap is brown instead of white. They are also called Italian brown mushrooms and are available in many supermarkets.

4 Servings — 113 Calories per serving

½ ounce dried porcini or other dried imported mushrooms
1 tablespoon olive oil
10 ounces cremini or white button mushrooms, coarsely chopped
1 cup chopped onion
1 garlic clove, crushed through a press
1 can (28 ounces) Italian-style plum tomatoes, with their juices
1 teaspoon salt
¼ teaspoon freshly ground black pepper
4 Italian (flat leaf) parsley leaves, for garnish

1. Combine the porcini and 3 cups water in a small saucepan. Bring to a boil, remove from the heat, cover and let stand 30 minutes. Carefully strain through a very fine mesh sieve or a sieve lined with a paper towel that has been dampened and squeezed dry; reserve the liquid. Rinse the porcini well to remove any sand or grit. Chop the porcini and set aside.

2. Heat the oil in a large wide nonaluminum saucepan or Dutch oven. Add the chopped cremini or white button mushrooms and the onion. Cook over medium-high heat, stirring often, until the mushrooms and onion are tender and any moisture has cooked off, about 10 minutes. Add the garlic and cook 1 minute longer.

3. Purée the tomatoes in a food processor or blender. Add to the saucepan along with the reserved porcini liquid and chopped porcini. Bring to a boil, reduce the heat to medium and cook, uncovered, for 10 minutes.

4. Season with the salt and pepper. Ladle into bowls and garnish each serving with a parsley leaf.

Seafood Soup

Seafood soup, or *zuppa di pesce* in Italian, is a stewlike soup, much like the French *boullabaisse,* which is naturally low in calories. It is a versatile way to use a combination of clams, mussels, shrimp and firm-fleshed white fish, such as cod, halibut, shark or other fish, and is a great treat for family and company alike. Saffron, the stamen of the crocus flower, is what gives the dish its distinctive flavor.

Because the soup is so light, you can afford the extra 48 calories one crisp garlic toast will add (see Crostini, p. 21). Place on the bottom of each bowl and ladle the soup over it.

4 Servings | 200 Calories per serving

1/8 teaspoon ground saffron or 4 or 5 saffron threads
1/2 cup boiling water
1/2 cup sliced onion
1 garlic clove, crushed through a press
1 tablespoon olive oil
1/2 cup dry white wine
1 can (28 ounces) Italian-style plum tomatoes, with their juices
1 strip of orange zest (2 × 1/2 inch)
12 littleneck clams or mussels or half clams and half mussels, rinsed and scrubbed
8 to 10 ounces fish steak, such as halibut, cod, and/or mako, skinned, boned and cut into 4 pieces
4 large shrimp (about 3 ounces), shelled and deveined
2 tablespoons chopped fresh basil or Italian (flat leaf) parsley
Freshly ground black pepper

1. Combine the saffron and boiling water; let stand 10 minutes. Combine the onion, garlic and oil in a large wide nonaluminum saucepan or Dutch oven. Cook over medium-low heat, stirring occasionally, until the onion is soft, about 5 minutes.

2. Add the wine and bring to a boil; boil 1 minute. Add the tomatoes with their juices, orange zest and saffron and its soaking liquid. Bring to a boil, breaking up the tomatoes with the side of a large spoon. Reduce the heat to low, cover and simmer 15 minutes.

3. First add the clams or mussels to the broth; then top with the pieces of fish and the shrimp. Sprinkle the basil on top. Cover and cook over medium-low heat until the fish and shrimp are opaque to the center and the shellfish have opened, about 5 minutes. Discard any shellfish that do not open.

4. To serve, spoon the seafood into shallow soup bowls, distributing evenly. Season the broth with a grinding of pepper and ladle over the seafood.

Tortellini in Brodo

Look for good-quality tortellini, which are chubby little rings of pasta stuffed with cheese or meat, in the refrigerated section of your supermarket. Often there will be a choice of plain or spinach pasta. Use a richly flavored chicken broth, preferably homemade. To turn this into a main dish soup, double the amount of tortellini. A handful of tender greens—spinach, arugula or watercress leaves—can also be added for color.

6 Servings — 186 Calories per serving (see Note)

1 package (10 ounces) refrigerated or frozen tortellini
7 cups unsalted or reduced-sodium chicken broth
2 tablespoons grated Parmesan cheese

1. Cook the tortellini according to the package directions. Meanwhile, heat the chicken broth in a medium saucepan.

2. When they are just done, drain the tortellini and add to the broth. Bring to a gentle boil.

3. Ladle into soup bowls and sprinkle 1 teaspoon grated Parmesan cheese over each serving.

NOTE *The calorie count here is based on cheese tortellini.*

Fresh Vegetable Soup

Start with a good broth, either one you have made yourself or a good-quality canned broth. Use at least 6 different vegetables, increasing the amount of some if all of the suggested vegetables are not available.

Since the crostini are optional, they are not included in the calorie count. Keep in mind that each garlic toast will add another 48 calories per slice.

6 Servings — 164 Calories per serving

2 tablespoons olive oil
1 cup diced (1/4 inch) peeled carrot
1 cup sliced (1/2 inch) fresh green beans
1 cup sliced (1/2 inch) asparagus
1 cup diced (1/2 inch) scrubbed red potatoes
1/2 cup diced (1/4 inch) well-washed leek (white part only)
1/2 cup diced (1/4 inch) red onion
1/2 cup sliced celery
1/2 cup fresh or thawed frozen green peas
8 cups unsalted or reduced-sodium chicken broth
2 cups packed shredded fresh escarole or spinach
1/4 teaspoon salt, or to taste
Freshly ground black pepper
6 Crostini (p. 21, optional)
2 tablespoons grated Parmesan cheese

1. Heat the olive oil in a large wide saucepan or Dutch oven. Add the carrot, green beans, asparagus, potatoes, leek, red onion, celery and peas. Cook over medium-low heat, stirring occasionally, until the vegetables begin to soften, about 10 minutes.

2. Add the chicken broth and escarole and simmer 20 minutes. Season with the salt and a grinding of pepper.

3. Place a crostini in each soup plate. Ladle the soup over it, distributing the vegetables evenly. Sprinkle 1 teaspoon of Parmesan cheese over each serving.

Potato and Garlic Soup

4 Servings — 147 Calories per serving

4 to 5 cups chicken broth, preferably unsalted
2 cups diced peeled potatoes
2 tablespoons minced pancetta, trimmed prosciutto or bacon
1 tablespoon olive oil
½ cup finely chopped onion
2 garlic cloves, crushed through a press
⅛ teaspoon freshly ground black pepper
4 teaspoons grated Parmesan cheese

1. In a large saucepan, cook 4 cups of the chicken broth and the potatoes, covered, over medium heat until the potatoes are tender, about 20 minutes.

2. Meanwhile, in a small skillet, cook the pancetta in the olive oil over medium-low heat until lightly browned, about 5 minutes. Add the onion and cook, stirring often, until golden, about 5 minutes. Add the garlic and cook 2 minutes longer.

3. Using a slotted spoon, transfer half of the potatoes to a food processor. Add about 1 cup of the chicken broth. Process until smooth. Stir the purée back into the saucepan. Add the cooked pancetta mixture to the saucepan. Cover and cook over low heat 10 minutes, adding additional broth for a thinner soup. Season with the pepper.

4. To serve, ladle into bowls and sprinkle each with 1 teaspoon of the grated Parmesan cheese.

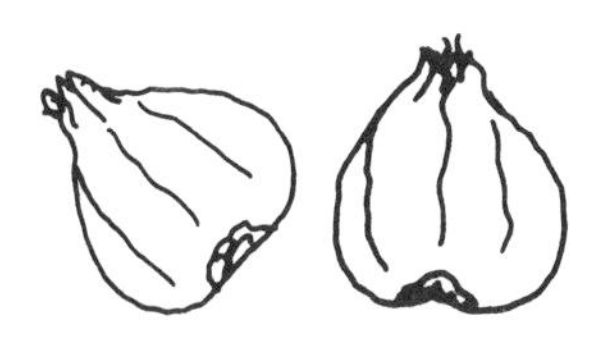

Chapter Three

PASTA

To most Italians, a meal is not complete without a small plate of pasta served as a first course, or *primi piatti.* On the other hand, we Americans tend to like to dig into heaping mounds of pasta as a main course. The good news is that even if you're eating a lighter, healthier diet, you can still enjoy pasta as often as you like, as long as the amount you eat is within bounds and the meal is balanced with other nutritious foods.

Pasta itself is largely composed of healthy complex carbohydrates. It is the heavy cream, butter and large amounts of oil in the sauce, however, that can send an otherwise lean dish up toward the stratosphere in terms of calories. We now know that it is not necessary to depend on the saturated fats in reduced heavy cream or extra knobs of sweet butter to make a dish palatable. Pasta can be sauced as elaborately as you like, as long as the ingredients are lean—seafood or an array of steamed vegetables bound with the juice of fresh chopped tomatoes, mushrooms. Even meat can be used, as long as the cuts are low in fat and its prime purpose is for flavor, not for bulk. The amount of olive oil can be reduced by ladling out a small amount of the flavorful pasta cooking water and using it to moisten the drained pasta—an old trick I borrowed from my grandmother.

Each ounce of uncooked pasta contains roughly 70 calories. If you can hold yourself down to 3 ounces per serving, you'll generally be fine, though some richer sauces are more demanding. All the recipes in this chapter were calculated at 400 calories or less.

Besides being healthful, pasta is a convenient food that can make the transformation from pantry to platter in less than 30 minutes. And the variety is endless. This collection contains everything from Spaghetti with Broccoli and Red Onion, Rotelle with Eggplant and Beef Sauce and Perciatelli with Pancetta and Arugula to Linguine with Shrimp Sauce, Linguine with Pesto Sauce and a healthful Zucchini and Carrot Sauce.

Match the shape of the pasta with the cut of the vegetable.

- With penne or other long tubular pasta use asparagus, green beans or carrot sticks, cut the same length as the penne.
- With spaghetti use coarsely shredded or finely chopped vegetables that will cling to the pasta so you can taste some of the vegetable with every forkful of pasta.
- With tubettini or other short tubular pasta use diced vegetable cut the same width and length as the pasta shape.
- Thin pasta sauces are best served on a broad pasta shape that will hold the sauce on its surface. A good example is linguine with seafood sauce or rigatoni with meat sauce.

SHAPES

FARFALLE	butterflies
PENNE	tubular shapes, cut diagonally on the ends to resemble a pen point
CONCHIGLIE	shells
DITALINI	short, straight cut tubes; used in minestrone
FUSILLI	corkscrew twists
ORECCHIETTE	small curved discs that look like "little ears"
RADIATORI	short deep-ridged accordionlike shapes
RIGATONI	large, ridged pasta tubes
PERCIATELLI	twice as thick as spaghetti, hollow in the center
PASTINA	the tiniest pasta, used mostly in soups
ROTELLE	fat short spirals, also called "wheels"
ZITI	long narrow tubes with a smooth surface

Rotelle with Eggplant and Beef Sauce

With little more than an ounce of meat per person added for flavor (as well as for valuable protein and B vitamins), this sauce gets its body and substance from low-calorie eggplant. Red bell pepper and tomato, also light vegetables, add color and complexity.

5 Servings — 393 Calories per serving

1/3 pound ground sirloin (90% lean)
2 tablespoons olive oil
1/4 cup chopped onion
1/2 cup diced (1/4 inch) red bell pepper
1 small eggplant (about 12 ounces), peeled and cut into 1/2-inch dice
1/3 cup beef broth, preferably unsalted
1 cup coarsely chopped fresh or drained canned tomato
1 garlic clove, crushed through a press
1/4 teaspoon salt
1/8 teaspoon freshly ground black pepper
12 ounces rotelle, or a tubular pasta, such as penne
1 tablespoon grated Parmesan cheese

1. Cook the ground beef in a large nonstick skillet over medium-high heat, crumbling the meat with the side of a spoon until browned, about 10 minutes. Transfer the browned ground beef to a strainer to drain off the fat.

2. Wipe out the skillet, add the olive oil and heat over medium heat. Add the onion and bell pepper; stir to coat with the oil. Add the eggplant, raise the heat to high and cook, stirring often, 5 minutes. Add the beef broth and cook, stirring often, until the broth is absorbed, about 5 minutes.

3. Add the cooked ground beef, chopped tomato and garlic. Cover, reduce the heat to medium and cook until the eggplant is tender, about 10 minutes. Uncover and cook until some of the liquid is evaporated and the sauce is slightly thickened, about 3 minutes. Season with the salt and pepper.

4. Meanwhile, cook the rotelle in a large pot of boiling salted water until al dente, or firm to the bite, 10 to 12 minutes; drain well. Transfer the pasta to a large serving bowl. Top with the sauce and toss. Sprinkle the Parmesan cheese over the top and serve.

Spaghettini with Browned Garlic

The simplest foods are frequently the most satisfying. A pantry stocked with spaghettini, olive oil and garlic is all one needs on hand to make this robust, classic pasta dish at practically a moment's notice.

4 SERVINGS — 381 CALORIES PER SERVING

2 tablespoons extra virgin olive oil
1 tablespoon thin slices of garlic (about 4 cloves)
½ teaspoon crushed hot red pepper, or to taste
12 ounces spaghettini (thin spaghetti)
2 tablespoons coarsely chopped Italian (flat leaf) parsley

1. Heat the olive oil in a small skillet over low heat until warm. Add the garlic and hot pepper and cook, stirring, until the garlic is soft, 3 to 5 minutes; do not brown.

2. Meanwhile, cook the spaghettini in a large pot of boiling salted water until al dente, or firm to the bite, 6 to 8 minutes. Ladle about ¼ cup of the pasta cooking liquid into a large serving bowl. Drain the pasta and add to the serving bowl. Top with the garlic and pepper-infused oil. Toss the spaghettini until coated with the oil. Sprinkle on the parsley and serve at once.

Spaghetti with Bell Pepper Strips and Garlic

4 SERVINGS — 388 CALORIES PER SERVING

2 tablespoons olive oil
1 red bell pepper or ½ red bell pepper and ½ yellow bell pepper, cut into thin (¼-inch) lengthwise strips
1 garlic clove, finely chopped
1 teaspoon fresh thyme or ⅛ teaspoon dried
Freshly ground black pepper
12 ounces spaghetti
1 tablespoon grated Parmesan cheese

1. Heat the olive oil in a small skillet. Add the pepper strips and cook over medium heat, stirring occasionally, until the edges begin to brown, about 5 minutes. Add the garlic and thyme, reduce the heat to low and cook, stirring, 1 minute. Add a generous grinding of black pepper; set aside until ready to serve.

2. Cook the spaghetti in a large pot of boiling salted water until al dente, or firm to the bite, 8 to 10 minutes. Ladle about ¼ cup of the pasta cooking liquid into a large serving bowl. Drain the pasta and add to the serving bowl. Top with the red pepper mixture and the Parmesan cheese. Toss the spaghetti until combined. Serve at once.

Spaghetti with Broccoli and Red Onion

In this recipe, the small florets of broccoli simmer along with the spaghetti during the last few minutes of cooking to save you a pot to clean. In addition, the broccoli absorbs the tasty pasta cooking liquid, making it juicy and tender.

4 Servings — 400 Calories per serving

1½ tablespoons olive oil
1 medium red onion, thinly sliced
12 ounces spaghetti
2 cups fresh broccoli florets (about 1-inch-long pieces)
2 tablespoons grated Parmesan cheese

1. Heat the olive oil in a small skillet. Add the onion and cook over medium-low heat, stirring, until softened, about 3 minutes. Set aside.

2. Cook the spaghetti in a large pot of boiling salted water 6 minutes. Stir in the broccoli and cook until the broccoli is tender and the pasta is al dente, or firm to the bite, about 3 minutes longer.

3. Ladle about ¼ cup of the pasta cooking liquid into a large serving bowl. Drain the pasta and add to the serving bowl. Add the red onion and Parmesan cheese. Toss and serve at once.

Pasta with Broccoli Rabe

In Italy, a curved pasta called *orecchiette,* or "little ears," is served with broccoli rabe, but other fat, chunky shapes, such as shells or a deeply ridged pasta called *radiatori,* are also good choices. If broccoli rabe is unavailable, substitute regular broccoli cut into florets. Romano cheese, slightly sharper than Parmesan, is traditionally served with this dish.

6 Servings — 344 Calories per serving

1 bunch of broccoli rabe (about 1¼ pounds) or 1 bunch of broccoli
2 tablespoons extra virgin olive oil
2 teaspoons minced garlic (about 2 cloves)
Pinch of crushed hot red pepper, or more to taste
1 pound pasta shells, orecchiette or radiatori
1 tablespoon grated Romano cheese

1. Cut the broccoli rabe, including stalks, into 1-inch lengths. If using broccoli, cut into small florets with 1 inch of the stems. There will be 3 to 4 cups.

2. Heat the olive oil in a small skillet over low heat until warm, about 30 seconds. Add the garlic and hot pepper and cook, stirring, until the garlic is soft, about 3 minutes; do not brown.

3. Cook the pasta in a large pot of boiling salted water, 5 minutes. Stir in the broccoli rabe and cook, stirring, until the pasta is al dente, or firm to the bite, and the broccoli rabe is very tender, 8 to 10 minutes longer.

4. Ladle about ½ cup of the pasta cooking liquid into a large serving bowl. Drain the pasta and broccoli rabe and add to the serving bowl. Drizzle the garlic oil over the pasta, sprinkle the cheese on top and toss. Serve at once.

Perciatelli with Pancetta and Arugula

Perciatelli is a long, fat, hollow spaghetti-type pasta; if it is not available, linguine is very good in this dish. The tiny amount of pancetta—a cured, unsmoked Italian bacon—adds a lot of flavor for a minimum of calories. If both pancetta and prosciutto are unavailable, substitute Black Forest ham or any other tasty ham.

4 SERVINGS — 356 CALORIES PER SERVING

1 tablespoon olive oil
¼ cup slivered red bell pepper
1 thin slice of pancetta or prosciutto, minced (about 1 tablespoon)
1 tablespoon thinly sliced garlic
12 ounces perciatelli or linguine
1 bunch of arugula, stemmed, trimmed and drained (about 2 cups lightly packed); watercress can be substituted

1. In a large skillet, preferably nonstick, combine the olive oil, red pepper, pancetta and garlic. Cook over medium-low heat until the garlic is golden and the pepper is tender, about 5 minutes. Remove from the heat, cover and keep warm.

2. Meanwhile, cook the perciatelli in a large pot of boiling salted water until al dente, or firm to the bite, 10 to 12 minutes. Ladle about ¼ cup of the pasta cooking liquid into a large serving bowl. Drain the pasta.

3. Stir the arugula into the pasta cooking liquid in the serving bowl just until wilted. Add the cooked pasta and toss to blend. Drizzle the red pepper and oil mixture over the pasta, toss gently and serve.

– *Farfalle with Summer Vegetables and Creamy Fresh Tomato Sauce* –

Farfalle, or butterfly-shaped pasta, sometimes called bow ties, is wonderful in this dish, but penne or rotelle is also good. The skim milk in this chunky fresh plum tomato sauce gives it a rich, creamy texture without the calories or fat of cream. An assortment of fresh vegetables adds color, flavor, volume and vitamins with no fat.

5 Servings — 344 Calories per serving

1 tablespoon olive oil
½ cup chopped onion
1 garlic clove, crushed through a press
1½ pounds fresh plum tomatoes, chopped (about 3 cups)
½ cup skim milk
¼ teaspoon salt
⅛ teaspoon freshly ground black pepper
1 medium carrot
1 yellow summer squash (about 5 ounces)
1 zucchini (about 5 ounces)
¼ pound fresh green beans
12 ounces farfalle, penne or rotelle
2 tablespoons slivered fresh basil (optional)
1 tablespoon grated Parmesan cheese

1. Heat the olive oil in a large nonstick skillet. Add the onion and cook over medium-low heat, stirring occasionally, until tender, 3 to 5 minutes. Add the garlic and cook 30 seconds. Add the tomatoes, raise the heat to medium, and cook, stirring often, until the sauce is thickened, 15 to 20 minutes. Stir in the milk and cook, stirring, 5 minutes. Season with the salt and pepper.

2. Peel the carrot. Cut the carrot, summer squash and zucchini into strips about 1½ inches long and ¼ inch wide; keep the vegetables in separate piles. Cut the green beans into 1½-inch lengths. There should be about 1 cup of each vegetable.

3. Cook the pasta in a large pot of boiling salted water 6 minutes; do not drain. Add the carrot and green beans to the pasta and cook 6 minutes, or until the pasta is almost tender, but still has a little too much firmness in the center. Add the summer squash and zucchini and cook 2 minutes longer, or until the vegetables are tender and the pasta is al dente. Drain into a colander.

4. Immediately transfer the pasta and vegetables to a deep platter. Pour the sauce over the top, sprinkle on the basil and cheese and serve.

Ditalini with Fresh Chopped Tomatoes

This is a wonderful dish for midsummer when tomatoes are at their best. Serve the pasta hot with the raw sauce or make ahead and serve at room temperature.

4 Servings — 391 Calories per serving

1½ pounds ripe fresh tomatoes, coarsely chopped (about 3 cups)
1½ tablespoons olive oil
2 tablespoons chopped fresh basil or Italian (flat leaf) parsley
1 garlic clove, crushed through a press
¼ teaspoon salt
12 ounces ditalini or other small pasta—tubettini, conchigliette or elbows

1. In a large serving bowl, combine the tomatoes, olive oil, basil, garlic and salt; stir to blend. Let stand while the pasta is cooking.

2. Cook the pasta in a large pot of boiling salted water until al dente, or firm to the bite, about 10 minutes. Drain at once and immediately add the hot pasta to the tomato mixture. Toss. Serve hot or at room temperature.

Chick Peas and Pasta

Some people make this more classic combination of ceci, or chick peas, and pasta as a soup. Here it is prepared as a pasta with ceci and tomato sauce. It is a soul-satisfying and nourishing dish that is very low in fat.

4 Servings — 392 Calories per serving

1 tablespoon plus 2 teaspoons olive oil
½ cup chopped onion
1 garlic clove, crushed through a press
1 can (19 ounces) chick peas, rinsed and drained
1 teaspoon fresh oregano or ¼ teaspoon dried
¼ teaspoon coarsely ground black pepper
¼ teaspoon crushed hot red pepper
1 bay leaf
1 can (28 ounces) Italian-style plum tomatoes, with their juices
2 cups elbow macaroni or small tubular pasta
1 tablespoon grated Parmesan cheese

1. Heat the olive oil in a large skillet. Add the onion and cook over medium-low heat, stirring occasionally, until tender, 3 to 5 minutes. Add the garlic and cook 1 minute longer.

2. Add the chick peas, oregano, black pepper, hot pepper and bay leaf. Cook, stirring, and crushing half of the chick peas with the back of a spoon, until heated through, about 5 minutes. Add the tomatoes with their juices. Bring to a boil over medium-high heat, stirring and breaking up the tomatoes with the side of a large spoon. Reduce the heat to medium-low, cover and simmer 10 minutes.

3. Meanwhile, cook the pasta in a large pot of boiling salted water until al dente, or firm to the bite, about 10 minutes. Drain and transfer to a large serving bowl.

4. Add the chick pea and tomato sauce to the pasta and toss to blend. Sprinkle the cheese over the top and serve.

Pasta Shells with Winter Vegetables

Cauliflower, broccoli, carrot—even chunks of potato and butternut squash—are delicious tossed with freshly cooked pasta. And they impart a feeling of fullness and satisfaction with a minimum of calories. Here they are bound together by garlic that has been slowly cooked in chicken broth and then mashed into a paste.

6 Servings — 392 Calories per serving

12 garlic cloves, peeled
¾ cup unsalted or reduced-sodium chicken broth
2 tablespoons olive oil
1 pound pasta shells, wagon wheels or rotelle
1 cup thinly sliced peeled carrots
1 cup diced (½ inch) peeled sweet potato or butternut squash
1 cup diced (½ inch) unpeeled red potatoes
1 cup broccoli florets
1 cup cauliflower florets

1. In a small saucepan, combine the garlic and chicken broth. Bring to a boil, reduce the heat to low, cover and cook until the garlic is very soft, about 20 minutes. Remove from the heat, uncover and let cool slightly. Transfer the garlic and broth to a food processor and purée until smooth. Add the olive oil and purée until blended.

2. Cook the pasta in a large pot of boiling salted water 3 minutes; do not drain. Add the carrots, sweet potato and red potatoes to the pasta and boil 5 minutes. Add the broccoli florets and cauliflower florets and boil 3 to 5 minutes longer, or until the pasta is al dente and the vegetables are tender. Ladle ½ cup of the pasta cooking liquid into a large serving bowl. Drain the pasta and vegetables.

3. Add the pasta and vegetables to the serving bowl. Scrape the garlic purée over the pasta and toss to mix. Serve at once.

Vegetable Lasagne

This streamlined but flavorful version of lasagne is made without meat and with more vegetable and low-fat ricotta filling than noodles.

6 Servings — 321 Calories per serving

2 teaspoons olive oil
¼ pound fresh mushrooms, thinly sliced (about 1 cup)
½ cup finely chopped onion
½ cup finely chopped peeled carrot
1 garlic clove, crushed through a press
2 cups packed washed, trimmed and coarsely chopped fresh spinach (about 5 ounces)
⅛ teaspoon salt
⅛ teaspoon freshly ground black pepper
1 cup reduced-fat or part-skim ricotta cheese
2 tablespoons chopped Italian (flat leaf) parsley or fresh basil
2 tablespoons grated Parmesan cheese
1 recipe Easy Marinara Sauce (p. 78) or 2 cups of your favorite pasta sauce
6 lasagne noodles, cooked and drained
1½ cups coarsely shredded part-skim mozzarella cheese (6 ounces)

1. Heat the olive oil in a large nonstick skillet. Add the mushrooms, onion and carrot and cook over medium heat, stirring, until the carrot is tender, 8 to 10 minutes. Raise the heat to high and cook, stirring, until any excess moisture is evaporated. Add the garlic and cook 1 minute. Stir in the spinach until blended. Cover and cook over low heat until the spinach is wilted, about 3 minutes. Season with the salt and pepper. Remove from the heat.

2. In a food processor, combine the ricotta cheese, parsley and 1 tablespoon of the Parmesan cheese. Purée until smooth and creamy. Set the flavored ricotta aside.

3. Preheat the oven to 350° F. Select a shallow baking dish about 9 × 13 inches. Spread ½ cup of the tomato sauce in the bottom of the dish. Cover the bottom with 2 of the lasagne noodles, cutting to fit, if necessary. Spoon the spinach mixture over the pasta; spread out in an even layer. Sprinkle ¼ cup of the mozzarella cheese over the filling. Top with 2 more of the lasagne noodles.

4. Spread the flavored ricotta over the noodles and sprinkle another ¼ cup mozzarella cheese over the ricotta. Top with the last 2 lasagne noodles. Pour the remaining tomato sauce over the top layer of noodles. Sprinkle with the remaining 1 cup shredded mozzarella and the remaining 1 tablespoon grated Parmesan cheese.

5. Cover the dish with aluminum foil and bake 30 minutes. Uncover and bake 20 minutes, or until the top is bubbly and browned. Let stand 10 minutes before serving.

Penne with Tomato Sauce

6 Servings 350 Calories per serving

2 tablespoons extra virgin olive oil
1/4 cup finely chopped onion
1 can (28 ounces) Italian-style plum tomatoes, with their juices, or 3 cups peeled and chopped vine-ripened tomatoes
1 small garlic clove, crushed through a press
1/4 teaspoon salt
1/8 teaspoon freshly ground black pepper
1 pound penne or other tubular pasta
1/2 cup chopped fresh basil (optional)

1. Heat the olive oil in a large skillet. Add the onion and cook over medium-low heat, stirring occasionally, until tender, about 5 minutes; do not brown. Add the tomatoes with their juices and the garlic. Bring to a simmer, breaking up the tomatoes with the side of a large spoon. Simmer over medium-low heat, stirring occasionally, until the sauce is slightly thickened, about 25 minutes. Season with the salt and pepper.

2. Cook the pasta in a large pot of boiling salted water until al dente, or firm to the bite, 10 to 12 minutes; drain well. In a large serving bowl, toss the pasta with just enough sauce to coat lightly. Add the basil and toss to blend. Spoon the remaining sauce on top and serve.

Penne with Arugula and Red Onion

4 Servings — 392 Calories per serving

1 bunch of arugula
2 tablespoons extra virgin olive oil
½ cup thinly sliced red onion
1 garlic clove, crushed through a press
12 ounces penne or other tubular pasta
1 tablespoon grated Parmesan cheese

1. Trim any roots and thick stems from the arugula. Wash the arugula in several changes of cold water and drain well. There should be about 2 cups packed.

2. Heat the olive oil in a large skillet. Add the red onion and cook, stirring, until tender, about 5 minutes; do not brown. Add the garlic and cook 1 minute. Stir in the arugula leaves and cook, stirring, until wilted and coated with the oil, about 2 minutes.

3. Cook the penne in a large pot of boiling salted water until the pasta is al dente, or firm to the bite, about 10 minutes.

4. Ladle about ½ cup of the pasta cooking liquid into a large serving bowl. Drain the pasta and add to the serving bowl. Add the arugula mixture and toss. Sprinkle with the Parmesan cheese and serve.

Linguine with Clams or Mussels

Look for cultivated tiny clams and plump juicy mussels for this simple sauce, which is especially good served over linguine.

4 Servings 375 Calories per serving

1 teaspoon olive oil
¼ cup chopped onion
2 teaspoons minced garlic
½ cup dry white wine
1 can (14 ounces) Italian-style plum tomatoes, with their juices
1 bay leaf
1 strip of orange zest (2 × ½ inch)
1 teaspoon fresh thyme or ⅛ teaspoon dried
12 mussels, scrubbed and debearded, or littleneck clams or 6 of each
1 tablespoon coarsely chopped Italian (flat leaf) parsley
1 tablespoon coarsely chopped fresh basil (optional)
⅛ teaspoon freshly ground black pepper
12 ounces linguine or spaghetti, cooked until al dente

1. Heat the olive oil in a large deep nonaluminum skillet or Dutch oven with a tight-fitting lid. Add the onion and cook over low heat, stirring, until tender, about 5 minutes. Add the garlic and cook 1 minute longer.

2. Add the wine and bring to a boil; boil 1 minute. Add the tomatoes with their juices, bay leaf, orange zest and thyme. Bring to a boil, breaking up the tomatoes with the side of a large spoon. Reduce the heat to medium-low, cover and simmer 5 minutes.

3. Raise the heat to medium-high, add the mussels and/or clams to the simmering sauce, cover and cook 5 minutes, or until all the shellfish open. With a slotted spoon, remove the shellfish to a bowl. Discard any that do not open.

4. Retrieve the orange zest from the sauce and finely chop it along with the parsley and basil; set aside. Remove and discard the bay leaf. Heat the sauce to boiling. Season with the pepper.

5. Ladle some of the sauce into a shallow serving bowl and add the freshly cooked pasta. Spoon the shellfish over the pasta and ladle on the remaining sauce; the mixture will be and should be soupy. Sprinkle the chopped orange zest and herbs over the top. Serve at once in shallow soup bowls.

Variation

Linguine with Shrimp Sauce: Substitute 6 ounces shelled and deveined medium shrimp for the clams or mussels in the recipe above.

4 Servings — 399 Calories per serving

Linguine with Pesto Sauce

This reduced-fat version of the classic Italian basil sauce, *pesto,* is for when your garden is bursting with the lush, leafy herb, or when it is most affordable at the market. For a sharper flavor, use grated Pecorino Romano cheese (made from sheep's milk) instead of the more mellow Parmesan (made from cow's milk).

4 Servings — 400 Calories per serving

1 cup packed coarsely chopped fresh basil
¼ cup grated Parmesan cheese
3 tablespoons extra virgin olive oil
3 tablespoons unsalted or reduced-sodium chicken broth
1 garlic clove, chopped
¼ cup coarsely chopped walnuts
12 ounces linguine

1. In a food processor, combine the basil, Parmesan cheese, olive oil, chicken broth and garlic; purée until almost smooth. Add the walnuts and process 10 seconds. Set the pesto aside.

2. Cook the linguine in a large pot of boiling salted water until al dente, or firm to the bite, 10 to 12 minutes. Ladle out ½ cup of the pasta cooking water and reserve. Drain the pasta.

3. Immediately transfer the pasta to a large serving bowl. Stir the pasta cooking water into the pesto. Pour the sauce over the pasta, toss and serve.

Easy Marinara Sauce

For a chunky sauce, leave the tomatoes whole. For a smoother sauce, purée the tomatoes in a food mill or food processor before adding them to the sauce.

Makes about 2 cups — 74 Calories per 1/2 cup

1 tablespoon olive oil
¼ cup finely chopped onion
1 small garlic clove, crushed
1 can (28 ounces) Italian-style plum tomatoes, with their juices, puréed if desired
2 tablespoons chopped Italian (flat leaf) parsley or fresh basil
1 teaspoon minced fresh oregano or thyme or ⅛ teaspoon dried
¼ teaspoon salt
⅛ teaspoon freshly ground black pepper

1. Heat the olive oil in a large nonstick skillet. Add the onion and cook over medium-low heat, stirring, until tender, 3 to 5 minutes. Do not brown. Add the garlic and cook 1 minute longer.

2. Add the tomatoes with their juices. Bring to a boil, breaking up the tomatoes with the side of a large spoon if they have not been puréed. Simmer over medium heat, stirring occasionally, until slightly thickened, about 25 minutes. Stir in the parsley, oregano, salt and pepper.

Variations

Tomato and Mushroom Sauce: Cook 1 cup chopped white button mushrooms along with the onion in step 1.

78 Calories per ½ cup

Fiery Tomato and Red Pepper Sauce: Add 1/4 to 1/2 teaspoon crushed hot red pepper, to taste, along with the tomatoes in step 2.

74 Calories per 1/2 cup

Fresh Tomato Sauce

Use this sauce also to simmer skinless chicken breasts, fish fillets or large shelled and deveined shrimp. Serve with steamed rice to absorb the flavorful sauce.

Makes about 1 3/4 cups sauce, 4 servings — 60 Calories per serving

1 tablespoon olive oil
1/4 cup chopped onion
1 garlic clove, crushed through a press
3 cups chopped peeled fresh ripe tomatoes
1/8 teaspoon salt
Freshly ground black pepper
1 tablespoon chopped fresh basil (optional)

1. Heat the olive oil in a large nonstick skillet. Add the onion and cook over low heat, stirring occasionally, until tender, 3 to 5 minutes. Add the garlic and cook 1 minute longer.

2. Add the tomatoes and bring to a boil. Cook over medium heat, stirring occasionally, until the tomatoes are cooked down and the sauce is slightly thickened, about 20 minutes.

3. Season with the salt and a grinding of pepper. Stir in the basil just before serving.

Tomato and Meat Sauce

A good tomato and meat sauce is hard to beat. This one is traditional, made with whole pieces of meat, simmered for a long time until the sauce is dark in color and richly flavored. Only very lean meats, sirloin of beef and loin of pork, are used to keep the calories—and fat—as low as possible. This sauce freezes well.

MAKES 3½ CUPS — 151 CALORIES PER ½ CUP

½ pound lean sirloin steak, trimmed of all excess fat
½ pound lean pork tenderloin, trimmed of all excess fat
1 teaspoon olive oil
⅓ cup minced onion
1 garlic clove, crushed through a press
1 can (28 ounces) Italian-style plum tomatoes, chopped, with their juices
1 can (15 ounces) tomato sauce
1 can (6 ounces) tomato paste
1 bay leaf
¼ teaspoon dried oregano
¼ teaspoon salt
⅛ teaspoon freshly ground black pepper

1. In a large nonstick skillet, cook the steak and pork over medium-high heat, turning, until browned all over, about 10 minutes. Transfer the meat to a plate. Blot any fat from the skillet with a paper towel. Add ½ cup water to the skillet and bring to a boil, stirring and scraping up any browned bits from the bottom of the pan. Remove from the heat and set the drippings aside.

2. In a large wide nonaluminum saucepan or Dutch oven, heat the olive oil. Add the onion and cook over medium-low heat, stirring occasionally, until tender, 3 to 5 minutes. Add the garlic and cook 1 minute longer. Add the tomatoes and their juices, tomato sauce, tomato paste, reserved drippings from the skillet, bay leaf and oregano. Add the meats and any juices that have collected on the plate.

3. Bring to a simmer, reduce the heat to low and cook, uncovered, 1 to 1½ hours, or until the meats are very tender and the sauce is reduced and flavorful. Lift out the sirloin and pork with a long fork and coarsely chop. Return to the sauce. Season with the salt and pepper.

Zucchini and Carrot Sauce

This delicate sauce should be made just minutes before the pasta goes into the boiling water. It is best with fettuccine or thinner width noodles to match the narrow strips of orange carrot and green zucchini.

MAKES ABOUT 1½ CUPS SAUCE, 4 SERVINGS — 89 CALORIES PER SERVING

2 tablespoons olive oil
½ cup sliced red onion
1 cup coarsely shredded peeled carrot
½ cup unsalted or reduced-sodium chicken broth
1 cup coarsely shredded zucchini
1 garlic clove, crushed through a press
⅛ teaspoon salt
Freshly ground black pepper

1. Heat the olive oil in a medium skillet; add the onion and cook over low heat, stirring, until crisp-tender, about 2 minutes.

2. Add the carrot and chicken broth and bring to a boil. Simmer over medium-low heat 2 minutes. Add the zucchini and garlic and cook, stirring often, until the zucchini is barely tender, 1 to 2 minutes. Season with the salt and a generous grinding of pepper.

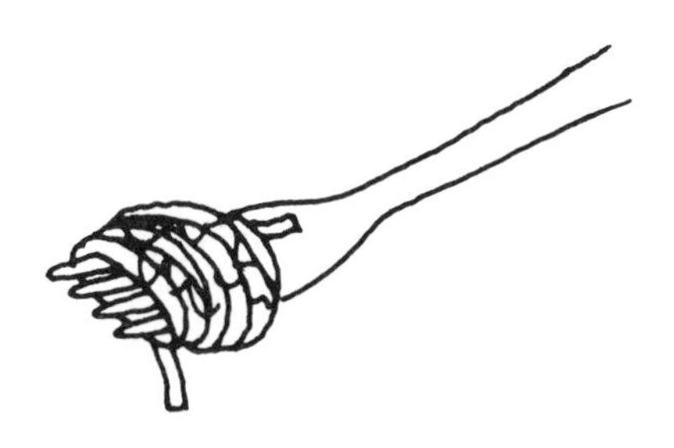

Chapter Four

VEGETABLES AND SALADS

For those interested in limiting their fat and cholesterol consumption and in consuming fewer calories without sacrificing taste and enjoyment, vegetables are number one on the list. You can splurge on vegetables, indulge in volume and still maintain a sensible diet. High in complex carbohydrates, providing a great source of fiber, vitamins and minerals, vegetables are so nutritious that United States Government health agencies now recommend that we consume five servings of vegetables each day, a number that may seem daunting to a generation that grew up on carrot sticks, boiled broccoli, iceberg lettuce salad and assorted frozen vegetables.

Italians take their produce seriously. In the smallest villages and the largest cities, open-air markets display a dazzling assortment of fruits and vegetables daily. And Italian cooking takes advantage of this agricultural richness, offering a wealth of ways to prepare both hot vegetables and salads. At the Italian table, in addition to their starring role in antipasto platters, vegetables, called *contorni,* are designed to complement a particular meat or fish, and they are considered an important part of the menu, not merely an extra dish.

In America, the demand for fresh vegetables is growing in leaps and bounds. Green markets proliferate in cities, and supermarket produce sections offer a much broader—and fresher—assortment of vegetables than ever before. Keep in mind, though, that fresh need not mean fussy.

From artichokes to zucchini, this chapter is bursting with good taste and an exhaustive selection of very simple recipes. Hot recipes like Baked Asparagus, New Potatoes with Sautéed Red Bell Peppers and Peas with Prosciutto and Onion and cool salads, such as Beet and Orange Salad, Plum Tomato, Red Onion and Mint Salad and Grilled Vegetable Salad, can be used in a variety of ways. Rice, potato and bean salads are also included here.

Because they are so lean, these tasty vegetables can add an extra course to your meal, either as a single first course or as part of a sampling of other antipasti. With a little extra cheese, a piece of leftover chicken or a little canned tuna, many of these would make delightful luncheon dishes. And, of course, they can turn any simple roasted or grilled meat or fish into an exceptional main course.

All the recipes in this chapter contain 175 calories or less. Many come in at under 100 calories per portion.

Tuscan Rice Salad

With the addition of slivers of lean cooked ham, roasted pork or smoked chicken, this appealing salad could easily be served as a light luncheon main dish.

8 Servings — 138 Calories per serving

1 cup long-grain white rice
1 cup diced (1/4 inch) peeled carrot
1 cup fresh or thawed frozen tiny green peas
2 tablespoons extra virgin olive oil
2 tablespoons red wine vinegar
1/2 teaspoon salt
1/8 teaspoon freshly ground black pepper
1/4 cup diced (1/4 inch) red onion
2 tablespoons finely chopped Italian (flat leaf) parsley

1. In a medium saucepan, bring 2 cups of water to a boil. Stir in the rice, reduce the heat to low and cover the pan. Cook 20 minutes, or until the rice is tender and all the water is absorbed. Fluff the rice with a fork and let cool to room temperature.

2. Meanwhile, place a vegetable steaming rack in a saucepan. Add 1 inch of water and bring to a boil. Arrange the carrot on the rack. Cover and steam 3 minutes. Add the peas to the steamer and steam 2 minutes longer, or until both vegetables are tender. Lift the steamer from the saucepan. Rinse the vegetables with cool water; drain.

3. In a large serving bowl, whisk together the olive oil, vinegar, salt and pepper until blended. Add the rice, carrot and peas, red onion and parsley. Toss to blend. Serve at room temperature.

Broccoli with Sautéed Garlic

Make cleanup easy by using the same pan for heating the oil and garlic that was used for steaming the broccoli.

4 Servings — 84 Calories per serving

1 bunch of broccoli (about 1 pound), trimmed and cut into narrow stalks for easy serving
2 tablespoons olive oil
2 garlic cloves, cut lengthwise into thin slices
4 lemon wedges

1. Place a vegetable steaming rack in a large wide saucepan or Dutch oven. Add 1 inch of water and bring to a boil. Arrange the broccoli in an even layer on the rack. Cover and steam until tender, 8 to 10 minutes.

2. Lift the steamer from the saucepan, discard the water and wipe the pan dry. Add the olive oil and garlic to the saucepan. Cook, stirring, over medium-low heat until the garlic sizzles gently and softens, 2 to 3 minutes.

3. Arrange the broccoli in a serving dish. Drizzle the oil and garlic over the broccoli. Garnish with the lemon wedges and serve.

Broccoli Rabe with Red Pepper Oil

Broccoli rabe, or rapini, is a popular low-calorie Italian green with a narrow stem and leafy tender flowers, and a pleasingly pungent, slightly bitter flavor. Like its cousin, ordinary broccoli, it is rich in vitamins A and C. Once an exotic vegetable, broccoli rabe can be found in many supermarkets as well as in Italian markets.

4 Servings — 88 Calories per serving

1½ pounds broccoli rabe, thick stem ends trimmed
2 tablespoons olive oil
¼ teaspoon crushed hot red pepper, or to taste

1. Bring a large saucepan filled with water to a boil. Add the broccoli rabe and return to a boil. Cook 5 minutes, or until almost tender. Drain immediately.

2. Meanwhile, in a large skillet, combine the olive oil and hot pepper. Heat over medium-low heat, stirring, until the oil is warmed and the pepper flakes sizzle, 2 to 3 minutes.

3. Add the drained broccoli rabe to the hot oil and toss to coat. Serve at once.

— *Green Beans and New Potatoes Vinaigrette* —

4 Servings | 175 Calories per serving

1 pound small red potatoes
½ pound fresh green beans
2 tablespoons olive oil
2 tablespoons red wine vinegar
¼ teaspoon salt
⅛ teaspoon freshly ground black pepper
½ cup thinly sliced red onion

1. Rinse the potatoes, scrubbing with a vegetable brush to remove any grit; rinse clean. Rinse and drain the green beans; trim the stem ends and cut into 1-inch lengths.

2. Cook the potatoes in a large pot filled with water until almost tender, 12 to 15 minutes. Add the green beans and cook until the potatoes and beans are both tender, about 5 minutes. Drain.

3. In a serving bowl, combine the oil, vinegar, salt and pepper. Whisk until blended. Add the potatoes, beans and red onion. Toss and serve.

Parmesan Baked Celery

This recipe for baked celery can also be prepared with fennel. Trim and chill the fennel first as directed in step 1 in the following recipe (p. 89). Either way, this is an excellent dish that is especially good with roasted chicken or baked fish.

4 Servings — 60 Calories per serving

1 large bunch of celery (about 1¼ pounds)
1 teaspoon olive oil
½ ounce Parmesan cheese in a chunk or 2 tablespoons grated Parmesan

1. Trim the base from the celery; remove and reserve the 4 large darker green outside stalks for another use. Cut off the top part of the remaining celery bunch about 6 inches up from the base. Reserve the top sections for another use.

2. Preheat the oven to 350° F. Using a sharp knife, divide the celery lengthwise into quarters. Arrange in a small baking dish. Drizzle the olive oil over the celery. Cover the dish tightly with aluminum foil and bake 1 hour, or until the celery is very tender when pierced with a skewer. Remove the dish from the oven; leave the oven on.

3. Remove the foil. Using a swivel-bladed vegetable peeler, remove thin curls of Parmesan from the chunk of cheese and distribute them evenly over the celery; or sprinkle on the grated cheese. Return the celery to the oven and bake, uncovered, until the cheese melts, about 10 minutes.

Braised Fennel with Parmesan Cheese

Fennel, also called anise, and known in Italy as *finocchio,* is crisp and like celery, which it resembles, is exceedingly light. Cooked fennel is soft to the bite with a pleasant, mellow licoricelike taste.

4 Servings — 21 Calories per serving

1 large fennel bulb (about 1 pound)
¼ cup unsalted or reduced-sodium chicken broth

2 teaspoons grated Parmesan cheese

1. Trim the base of the fennel bulb. Cut across the top to remove the darker green portions of the ribs and the fernlike tops. Using a sharp knife, cut the fennel lengthwise into quarters. Place the fennel in a large bowl and cover with ice water. Let stand 30 minutes before cooking.

2. Drain the fennel and arrange in a medium skillet. Add the chicken broth and bring to a boil. Cover and cook over low heat, uncovering occasionally to turn the fennel and to add small amounts of broth or water to keep the pan moist, until the fennel is tender when pierced with a skewer, about 25 minutes.

3. Uncover the skillet and boil off any excess broth. Transfer the fennel to a serving dish and sprinkle Parmesan cheese on top.

Braised Greens and Garlic with Vinegar

Use all of one type of green or mix several varieties in the same dish. This healthful combination is excellent served with a rich meat, such as pork, or one of the more flavorful fish, such as salmon.

4 Servings — 58 Calories per serving

2 pounds romaine lettuce, chicory (curly endive) and/or escarole
2 teaspoons olive oil
1 tablespoon thinly sliced garlic
1 tablespoon red wine vinegar

1. Rinse and trim the greens. Tear the leaves into 2-inch pieces. There will be about 12 cups.

2. In a large skillet or Dutch oven with a tight-fitting lid, combine ¼ cup water, 1 teaspoon of the oil and garlic. Cook over low heat, stirring often, until simmering. Cover and cook, stirring occasionally and adding small amounts of water if necessary, until the garlic is soft, about 10 minutes.

3. Gradually add the greens and toss until slightly wilted and coated with oil. Cover and cook over low heat, stirring once or twice, until the greens are tender, about 12 minutes. Uncover, raise the heat to medium and boil off the excess liquid. Sprinkle on the vinegar and the remaining 1 teaspoon olive oil, and stir to blend. Serve warm.

Marinated Grilled Vegetables

Let the season determine which vegetables to use. Summer vegetables, such as sweet baby eggplant, young zucchini and summer squash, wedges of red and yellow bell peppers and thick slices of sweet red onion, are especially good. All-season vegetables, like *shiitake* mushrooms, scallions and slices of Russet potato, also make excellent choices.

6 Servings — 80 Calories per serving

2 tablespoons extra virgin olive oil
1 tablespoon minced fresh oregano or ½ teaspoon dried
3 garlic cloves, bruised with side of a knife
At least 3 of the following vegetables:
2 baby eggplant, small zucchini and/or yellow squash, halved lengthwise
1 large red bell pepper and 1 large yellow bell pepper, cut into thick wedges, stems and seeds removed
4 thick slices of sweet red onion (see Note)
4 large shiitake *or white button mushrooms, stemmed*
1 large Russet potato, scrubbed and cut lengthwise into ¼-inch-thick slices
¼ teaspoon salt
Freshly ground black pepper
Lemon wedges

1. Combine the olive oil, oregano and garlic in a small bowl. Place the selected vegetables on a platter and drizzle the oil mixture over them. Season with the salt and a grinding of pepper. Cover and marinate at room temperature at least 30 minutes.

2. Light a hot fire in a grill or preheat your broiler. Grill the vegetables, turning them as needed, until evenly browned and tender, about 5 to 10 minutes per side, depending on the heat of the grill. If using an oven broiler, place the pan with the vegetables 2 to 3 inches from the heat source. Transfer the vegetables to a large platter as they are cooked.

3. Garnish with lemon wedges to squeeze over the grilled vegetables. Serve warm or at room temperature.

NOTE *Skewer the red onion slices with thin skewers or wooden toothpicks to hold the rings together.*

Peperonata

This mixture of red bell peppers, onion and tomatoes is excellent served as a side dish with meats, poultry and even eggs. It also makes a delicious sauce for pasta and is particularly compatible with the large-ridged rigatoni and corkscrew-shaped rotelle.

4 Servings — 106 Calories per serving

2 tablespoons olive oil
1 large onion, thinly sliced
4 red bell peppers, cut into thin strips
1 garlic clove, minced
1½ cups coarsely chopped peeled fresh tomatoes or 1 can (14 ounces) Italian-style plum tomatoes, chopped, with their juices
¼ teaspoon salt
⅛ teaspoon freshly ground black pepper
1 tablespoon finely chopped Italian (flat leaf) parsley
1 tablespoon red wine vinegar

1. Heat the olive oil in a large nonstick skillet. Add the onion and cook over medium-low heat, stirring occasionally, until the onion is tender, about 5 minutes. Add the bell peppers, raise the heat to high and cook, stirring often, until the peppers begin to brown around the edges. Add the garlic and cook 2 minutes.

2. Add the tomatoes. Bring to a boil, reduce the heat to medium-low and simmer, uncovered, until the tomato juices are reduced and the mixture is thickened, about 15 minutes.

3. Season with the salt and a grinding of pepper. Stir in the parsley and vinegar before serving.

Oven-Roasted Peppers

Serve this versatile dish hot with roasted chicken, broiled steak or pork cutlets, or offer it at room temperature as part of a buffet. With a splash of vinegar, it turns into a salad. Leftovers are good tossed with freshly cooked pasta or as a condiment on sandwiches.

4 Servings — 98 Calories per serving

1 red bell pepper, cut into 1-inch wedges
1 green bell pepper, cut into 1-inch wedges
1 large sweet yellow onion, cut into 1-inch wedges
4 whole garlic cloves, peeled
2 tablespoons olive oil
2 tablespoons finely chopped fresh parsley
1 tablespoon fresh lemon juice or red wine vinegar
1 teaspoon fresh thyme or 1/4 teaspoon dried
1/4 teaspoon salt
Freshly ground black pepper

1. Preheat the oven to 400° F. In a 9 × 13-inch shallow baking dish, combine the red and green peppers, the onion and garlic. Drizzle the olive oil over the vegetables.

2. Roast the vegetables, turning them every 15 minutes, until the edges of the peppers and onion are browned and the garlic is golden, about 45 minutes.

3. In a serving dish, toss the roasted vegetables with the parsley, lemon juice, thyme, salt and a grinding of pepper. Serve warm or at room temperature.

— *Baked Red Onions with Sage Bread Crumbs* —

Baking the onions converts their crisp texture and pungent taste into a completely different vegetable with a silky texture and sweet flavor. Sage, an herb with a very assertive flavor, adds a pleasant dusky counterpoint.

4 SERVINGS — 119 CALORIES PER SERVING

4 large red onions, peeled
1 tablespoon olive oil
1/4 cup coarse dry bread crumbs (preferably made from day-old Italian bread)
1/2 teaspoon dried sage
1/4 teaspoon salt
1/8 teaspoon freshly ground black pepper

1. Trim the base of each onion so that it will sit evenly. Trim about 1/2 inch from the top of each onion so that a flat surface showing the rings of onion is exposed. Arrange the onions in a small baking dish or pie plate.

2. Preheat the oven to 350° F. Drizzle 1 teaspoon of the olive oil over the onions. Cover tightly with aluminum foil and bake 1 hour, or until the onions are tender when pierced with a skewer.

3. Meanwhile, heat the remaining 2 teaspoons olive oil in a large nonstick skillet. Add the bread crumbs and the sage. Cook over medium-low heat, stirring often, until the crumbs are golden, about 5 minutes. Season with the salt and pepper.

4. When the onions are tender, remove them from the oven; leave the oven on. Add the crumbs to the baking dish and stir to coat with the pan juices. Carefully press the moistened bread crumbs on the tops of the onions, dividing evenly. Return to the oven and bake 10 minutes longer, or until the crumbs are golden. Serve warm or at room temperature.

— Roasted Potatoes with Garlic and Rosemary —

These crusty oven-roasted potatoes are irresistible, and they make a great substitute for fatty French fries. Make sure to use a rigid spatula to turn the potatoes carefully so that they brown evenly on both sides.

5 SERVINGS — 159 CALORIES PER SERVING

1½ pounds medium red potatoes, scrubbed and cut into ¼-inch-thick slices
2 tablespoons olive oil
1 garlic clove, thinly sliced
1 teaspoon minced fresh rosemary or ½ teaspoon dried
½ teaspoon salt
¼ teaspoon freshly ground black pepper

1. Preheat the oven to 400° F. In a 9 × 13-inch baking dish, toss the potatoes with the olive oil, garlic and rosemary. Spread the slices in an even layer.

2. Roast the potatoes 1 hour, or until they are evenly browned and crisp, carefully turning the slices with a wide spatula and rearranging them every 20 minutes. Season with the salt and pepper. Serve hot.

— New Potatoes with Sautéed Red Bell Peppers —

The skins on small (new) red potatoes are so tender they don't need peeling, and the potatoes themselves are so flavorful they need very little embellishment. Here they are simply tossed with sautéed slivers of red bell pepper with garlic and fresh parsley.

6 SERVINGS — 164 CALORIES PER SERVING

2 pounds small red or other new potatoes, scrubbed
2 tablespoons olive oil
¼ cup slivers (1 × ¼-inch pieces) red bell pepper
1 garlic clove, crushed
2 tablespoons chopped Italian (flat leaf) parsley

1. Cook the potatoes in a large saucepan of boiling water until tender when pierced with a skewer, about 20 minutes. Drain and set aside until cool enough to handle.

2. Heat the olive oil in a small nonstick skillet or saucepan. Add the bell pepper slivers and cook over medium heat, stirring often, until the edges begin to brown, about 5 minutes. Stir in the garlic and remove from the heat.

3. When the potatoes are cool enough to handle, halve them and place in a serving dish. Add the hot garlic oil and pepper mixture and the parsley; toss to coat. Serve warm or at room temperature.

Peas with Prosciutto and Onion

While it is a good idea to keep saturated fats to a minimum in any healthy diet, one thin slice of prosciutto adds just enough extra flavor but less than 2 grams of fat to this particular side dish. If prosciutto is not available, brown a slice of pancetta or bacon, drain off all the fat and then cut the meat into small dice. Sprinkle it over the cooked peas.

4 Servings — 91 Calories per serving

1 teaspoon olive oil
¼ cup finely chopped onion
1 thin slice of prosciutto, finely diced (about 1 tablespoon)
2 pounds fresh peas, shelled (about 2 ⅓ cups) or use 1 package (10 ounces) thawed frozen tiny peas

1. Heat the olive oil in a medium nonstick skillet with a tight-fitting lid. Add the onion and cook over medium heat, stirring occasionally, until tender but not browned, 3 to 5 minutes. Add the prosciutto and cook 2 minutes longer.

2. Add the peas to the skillet, cover and reduce the heat to medium-low. Cook 2 minutes. Uncover and taste. If the peas are not tender enough, cook, uncovered, 1 to 2 minutes longer.

— *Sautéed Mushrooms with Parsley and Garlic* —

4 Servings | 80 Calories per serving

2 tablespoons olive oil
10 ounces mushrooms, cut into 1/4-inch-thick slices
1 garlic clove, minced
2 tablespoons chopped Italian (flat leaf) parsley
1 teaspoon fresh thyme or 1/4 teaspoon dried
2 teaspoons fresh lemon juice
1/4 teaspoon salt
1/8 teaspoon freshly ground black pepper

1. Heat the olive oil in a large nonstick skillet over medium-high heat. Add the mushrooms and sauté, stirring, until browned and tender, about 10 minutes. Add the garlic and cook 1 minute longer.

2. Stir in the parsley and thyme. Sprinkle the lemon juice over the mushrooms and season with the salt and pepper. Serve hot.

— *Wilted Spinach with Olive Oil and Vinegar* —

4 Servings | 97 Calories per serving

2 pounds fresh spinach, rinsed well, stems removed, large leaves torn in half
2 tablespoons extra virgin olive oil
1 small garlic clove, crushed through a press
2 teaspoons red wine vinegar

1. Place a vegetable steaming rack in a large wide nonaluminum saucepan or Dutch oven. Add 1 inch of water and bring to a boil. Spread the spinach on the rack. Cover and cook until the spinach is wilted but still bright green, about 2 minutes.

2. Lift the steamer from the saucepan and discard the water. Put the steamed spinach in the saucepan, add the olive oil and garlic and cook over medium heat, stirring, just until heated through, 1 to 2 minutes. Remove from the heat and stir in the vinegar. Serve at once.

– *Zucchini Simmered with Tomatoes and Onion* –

This simple saucepan mixture of onion, zucchini and tomatoes provides an easy way to cook up zucchini that have grown just a little too large. Use canned tomatoes, if you must, but the dish is excellent when made with fresh, vine-ripened tomatoes.

6 Servings | 77 Calories per serving

1 tablespoon olive oil
1 large onion, cut into ½-inch chunks
1 garlic clove, crushed through a press
¼ teaspoon crushed hot red pepper, or to taste
2 pounds zucchini, cut into ½-inch dice
1 can (28 ounces) Italian-style plum tomatoes, with their juices, or 3 cups coarsely chopped fresh ripe tomatoes
¼ teaspoon salt
Freshly ground black pepper

1. Heat the olive oil in a large nonaluminum saucepan. Add the onion and cook over medium heat until golden, about 5 minutes. Add the garlic and hot pepper; cook 2 minutes longer.

2. Add the zucchini and the tomatoes with their juices. Bring to a boil over medium-high heat, stirring occasionally. Reduce the heat to medium-low, cover and cook 30 minutes, or until the zucchini is very tender.

3. Season with salt and a grinding of pepper. Serve hot or at room temperature. The flavors improve upon standing.

Zucchini Baked with Tomatoes

This foolproof dish can be made ahead and served warm or at room temperature. It is excellent with grilled fish.

4 Servings | 107 Calories per serving

½ large onion, thinly sliced
2 tablespoons olive oil
1¼ to 1½ pounds small zucchini, cut into ½-inch-thick diagonal slices
1 garlic clove, crushed through a press
1 teaspoon chopped fresh oregano or ¼ teaspoon dried
¼ teaspoon salt
⅛ teaspoon freshly ground black pepper
1 can (14 ounces) Italian-style plum tomatoes, coarsely cut up, with their juices
1 strip of orange zest (2 × ½ inch)

1. Preheat the oven to 400° F. In a shallow oval or rectangular 9 × 13-inch baking dish toss together the onion slices and olive oil until the onion is coated. Bake until the onion begins to brown, about 10 minutes.

2. Add the zucchini, garlic, oregano, salt and pepper; stir to blend. Bake 5 minutes longer.

3. Stir in the tomatoes with their juices and the strip of orange zest. Return the dish to the oven and bake until the tomatoes thicken slightly and the zucchini is tender, about 10 minutes. Serve hot or at room temperature.

Zucchini Sautéed with Onion and Lemon

The neutral flavor of zucchini makes it an especially versatile vegetable. Here it is sautéed with onion and lemon. If fresh lemon thyme is available, add a generous pinch of the leaves just before serving.

4 Servings | 91 Calories per serving

2 tablespoons olive oil, preferably extra virgin
½ cup diced (¼ inch) onion

1½ pounds small zucchini, cut into ¼-inch dice (about 4 cups)
1 teaspoon finely shredded lemon zest
1 tablespoon finely chopped Italian (flat leaf) parsley
1 teaspoon fresh lemon thyme leaves (optional)
¼ teaspoon salt
Freshly ground black pepper

1. Heat 1 tablespoon of the olive oil in a large nonstick skillet. Add the onion and cook over medium heat, stirring occasionally, until golden, about 5 minutes.

2. Add the zucchini and lemon zest. Cook, stirring often, until the zucchini are tender, 5 to 8 minutes. Add the parsley, thyme, salt and a grinding of pepper. Spoon into a serving dish and drizzle the remaining 1 tablespoon olive oil over the zucchini.

— *Green Beans with Garlic and Red Pepper Oil* —

Here is a lusty salad for garlic lovers. The crushed red pepper adds a fiery zip, and nothing is nicer when you're watching your diet than big flavors that pique your taste buds and satisfy your palate. Of course, the heat can be omitted if you prefer a tamer taste.

4 Servings — 109 Calories per serving

1½ pounds tender fresh green beans, ends trimmed
2 tablespoons olive oil
¼ to ½ teaspoon crushed hot red pepper, to taste
2 garlic cloves, crushed through a press
⅛ teaspoon salt

1. Bring a large saucepan almost filled with water to a boil. Add the green beans, cover and return to a boil. Uncover and cook, stirring occasionally, until the beans are tender, about 5 minutes.

2. Meanwhile, heat the olive oil in a small skillet. Add the hot pepper and cook over low heat 3 minutes. Add the garlic and cook, stirring, just until it begins to turn golden, 1 to 2 minutes. Immediately remove from the heat.

3. Drain the green beans and transfer to a serving bowl. Add the hot garlic oil and salt. Toss to coat and serve while hot.

Green Beans with Olive Oil and Basil

4 Servings | 109 Calories per serving

1½ pounds tender fresh green beans, ends trimmed
2 tablespoons extra virgin olive oil
¼ cup packed chopped fresh basil or 2 tablespoons chopped Italian (flat leaf) parsley

1. Bring a large saucepan of water to a boil. Add the beans, cover and return to a boil. Uncover and cook, stirring occasionally, until the beans are tender, about 5 minutes. Drain immediately.

2. In a large serving bowl, combine the beans, olive oil and basil. Toss to coat and serve.

Baked Asparagus

Once you have tasted baked asparagus you will never want to eat it any other way. The dry heat of the oven seems to intensify the asparagus flavor. A light dusting of grated Parmesan during the last 5 minutes of baking makes a nice variation. Each tablespoon of cheese will cost you 25 calories, but since asparagus is so light, you can probably afford it.

4 Servings | 43 Calories per serving

1 pound fresh asparagus, ends trimmed
1 tablespoon extra virgin olive oil
Freshly ground black pepper

1. Preheat the oven to 400° F. Arrange the asparagus spears in a 9 × 13-inch baking dish. Drizzle the olive oil over the asparagus and season with a grinding of pepper. Toss to coat.

2. Bake 10 minutes. Using tongs, rearrange the asparagus and turn them over so that they will cook evenly. Bake 2 to 5 minutes longer, or until tender. Serve warm or at room temperature.

Roasted Beets with Herb Oil

Oven-roasted beets have a deep, rich taste that far surpasses the flavor of beets prepared by the more conventional method of boiling them in plenty of water.

6 Servings | 82 Calories per serving

6 beets, 2 to 2½ inches in diameter (about 1¾ pounds)
2 tablespoons extra virgin olive oil
1 tablespoon chicken broth or water
¼ cup packed fresh parsley leaves
1 tablespoon chopped fresh basil or ½ teaspoon dried
1 teaspoon chopped fresh oregano or ¼ teaspoon dried
1 tablespoon fresh lime juice
1 garlic clove, crushed through a press
⅛ teaspoon salt
Sprigs of fresh parsley, for garnish

1. Preheat the oven to 350° F. Scrub the beets and trim the stems, leaving about 2 inches attached to the beet. Tightly wrap each beet individually in a square of aluminum foil. Place the wrapped beets directly on the oven rack, evenly spaced, and bake 1 to 1½ hours, or until they test tender when pierced with a skewer. Let the beets cool in the foil before unwrapping.

2. Meanwhile, in a food processor, combine the olive oil, chicken broth, parsley leaves, basil, oregano, lime juice, garlic and salt. Process until finely chopped and blended. Transfer the herb oil to a small bowl, cover with plastic wrap and set aside at room temperature until ready to serve.

3. When the beets are cool enough to handle, unwrap them, remove the stems and slip off the skins. Cut the beets into ¼-inch-thick slices and arrange on a large platter. Drizzle the herb oil over the beet slices and garnish with sprigs of parsley.

White Beans Italian Style

These savory beans are especially good with leg of lamb. If there are any leftover beans, add a little chopped parsley, celery and red onion and serve cold as a salad.

8 Servings | 170 Calories per serving

1½ cups dried cannellini (white kidney beans) or Great Northern beans (¾ pound), rinsed and picked over to remove any grit
2 cups unsalted or reduced-sodium chicken broth
4 large garlic cloves, bruised with side of a knife and peeled
2 sprigs of fresh sage with 8 to 10 leaves attached or 1 teaspoon dried
1 tablespoon olive oil, preferably extra virgin
1 small onion, halved
1 small celery rib with leafy top
½ teaspoon salt
2 tablespoons fresh lemon juice
¼ teaspoon freshly ground black pepper

1. In a large saucepan or Dutch oven, soak the beans in water to cover overnight. Or combine the beans with enough water to cover by 2 inches in a large saucepan, bring to a boil and boil 1 minute; remove the saucepan from the heat, cover and let stand 1 hour. Drain well.

2. Preheat the oven to 325° F. Place the beans in a heavy casserole with a lid or an enameled cast-iron pot. Add the chicken broth, garlic, sage, olive oil, onion, celery and salt; stir to mix.

3. Cover and bake 1 hour and 20 minutes, or until the beans are tender and most of the liquid is absorbed. Remove from the oven. Stir in the lemon juice and pepper.

Cannellini Beans with Escarole

Although I prefer the texture of cooked dried cannellini beans, canned cannellini (or white kidney beans) are certainly a suitable—and convenient—substitute. While this melange of beans and escarole is dressed like a salad, with oil and vinegar, it is really a vegetable side dish, good served with roasted veal, beef or lamb.

4 Servings | 169 Calories per serving

2 tablespoons olive oil
½ cup chopped onion
¼ cup chopped peeled carrot
1 garlic clove, crushed through a press
1 small head of escarole, rinsed well and torn into 1-inch pieces (4 cups)
2 tablespoons unsalted or reduced-sodium chicken broth or cold water
1 can (16 or 19 ounces) cannellini (white kidney beans), rinsed and drained
2 tablespoons red wine vinegar, or more to taste
Freshly ground black pepper

1. Heat 1 tablespoon of the olive oil in a large nonstick skillet with a tight-fitting lid. Add the onion and carrot and cook over medium heat, stirring occasionally, until the onion is tender, about 5 minutes. Add the garlic and cook 1 minute longer.

2. Stir in the escarole until slightly wilted and coated with the oil. Add the chicken broth, reduce the heat to low, cover and cook until the escarole is wilted and tender, about 5 minutes.

3. Add the beans, stirring gently to blend without crushing the beans. Add the remaining 1 tablespoon olive oil, the vinegar and a generous grinding of pepper. Serve warm.

Red Pepper and Fennel Salad

The slightly anise flavor of raw fennel is delicious in this brightly colored salad. If fennel is not available, use celery instead. For a little drama, add a few black olives just before serving.

4 Servings 93 Calories per serving

1½ pounds fennel bulb
2 medium red bell peppers, cut into ¼-inch strips
2 tablespoons olive oil
1 tablespoon fresh lemon juice
⅛ teaspoon salt
Freshly ground black pepper

1. Trim the stem end and any bruises from the outside of the fennel. If the tops are attached, cut off and reserve enough of the dark green, fernlike tops to equal 2 tablespoons when chopped; discard the remaining tops and stalks.

2. Halve the fennel bulb lengthwise and cut crosswise into thin slices. Place the fennel in a large bowl and cover with cold water; add a few ice cubes and refrigerate about 30 minutes, or until crisped.

3. Just before serving, drain the fennel and pat dry with paper towels. In a salad bowl, combine the fennel, finely chopped fennel tops and red pepper. Add the olive oil, lemon juice, salt and a grinding of pepper; toss and serve.

Red Cabbage and Tuna Salad

Stretching amounts of certain ingredients is one key to satisfaction when watching your diet, and here exceptionally low-calorie red cabbage stretches a can of tuna to feed four.

4 Servings 148 Calories per serving

4 cups shredded red cabbage (about 1 pound)
½ cup chopped scallions
¼ cup chopped Italian (flat leaf) parsley

1 can (6½ ounces) canned tuna, preferably packed in olive oil, drained
1 tablespoon olive oil
1 tablespoon fresh lemon juice
Freshly ground black pepper

1. In a large bowl, combine the red cabbage, scallions and parsley. Place the tuna in a small bowl and flake with a fork. Drizzle the olive oil and lemon juice over the tuna. Season with a generous grinding of pepper.

2. Add the tuna to the red cabbage and toss gently. Serve at room temperature.

Green Beans and Red Onion Salad

If you find young tender green beans, save preparation time by just trimming the stem ends. The tapered pointed ends are graceful and pretty and are quite edible, if the beans are fresh.

4 SERVINGS | 131 CALORIES PER SERVING

1½ pounds fresh green beans, ends trimmed
1 garlic clove, halved
1 large red onion, halved lengthwise and cut into thin slices
2 tablespoons extra virgin olive oil
¼ teaspoon salt
Freshly ground black pepper
¼ cup packed fresh basil (optional)

1. Fill a large saucepan with water; bring to a boil. Add the green beans, cover and cook until tender, about 5 minutes. Drain into a colander and rinse with cold water.

2. Rub the inside of a large salad bowl with the cut sides of the garlic. Add the green beans, red onion, olive oil, salt and a grinding of pepper. Add the basil. Toss gently and serve.

Green Bean Salad with Tomatoes

4 SERVINGS — 130 CALORIES PER SERVING

1½ pounds fresh green beans, ends trimmed
1 garlic clove, halved
4 large ripe plum tomatoes, quartered, seeded and cut into ¼-inch lengthwise strips
½ medium red onion, thinly sliced
2 tablespoons chopped fresh basil (optional)
2 tablespoons chopped fresh parsley
2 tablespoons olive oil
2 teaspoons fresh lemon juice
¼ teaspoon salt
⅛ teaspoon freshly ground black pepper

1. Fill a large saucepan with water; bring to a boil. Add the green beans, cover and cook until just tender, about 5 minutes. Drain into a colander and rinse with cold water.

2. Rub the inside of a large serving bowl with the cut sides of the garlic. Add the green beans, tomatoes, onion, basil, parsley, olive oil, lemon juice, salt and pepper. Toss and serve.

Bitter Greens with Parmesan Curls

Parmigiano-Reggiano, a favorite ingredient of the Italian kitchen, adds character to the simplest dishes. Buy it in chunks and keep it on hand for shaving onto a classic green salad like the following.

4 SERVINGS — 108 CALORIES PER SERVING

8 cups mixed bitter salad greens, such as arugula, chicory, Belgian endive, radicchio or romaine
2 tablespoons extra virgin olive oil
Freshly ground black pepper
1 small piece of Parmigiano-Reggiano (about ½ ounce), at room temperature

1. Rinse the greens and dry thoroughly; place in a large salad bowl. Drizzle the olive oil over the greens and add a grinding of pepper; toss gently to blend.

2. Using a swivel-bladed vegetable peeler, shave the cheese into short, thin slices, or "curls." Scatter over the salad to cover the surface entirely. Serve at once.

Beet and Orange Salad

Beet and orange is a classic flavor combination. The bright purple beets and orange colors are stunning together. Cook and slice the beets ahead and arrange the salad just before serving.

4 SERVINGS — 95 CALORIES PER SERVING

1 pound medium fresh beets (about 5)
½ cup thinly sliced red onion
2 strips of orange zest (2 × ½ inch each), cut into thin slivers
2 tablespoons red wine vinegar
1 tablespoon olive oil
1 garlic clove, bruised with side of a knife
¼ teaspoon salt
1 large seedless navel orange, peel and white pith removed, cut into thin rounds
1 tablespoon chopped Italian (flat leaf) parsley or fresh basil
Freshly ground black pepper

1. Trim all but 2 inches from the beet tops. Cook the beets in a large pot of boiling water until tender, 30 to 40 minutes; drain and let cool. (Or bake the beets according to the instructions for Roasted Beets with Herb Oil, p. 101.) Slip off the skins and remove the tops from the cooled cooked beets. Cut into ¼-inch slices.

2. In a medium bowl, combine the beets with the onion, orange zest, vinegar, olive oil, garlic and salt. Toss to blend.

3. Arrange the beets and orange slices in slightly overlapping circles on a serving plate. Sprinkle with the parsley and a grinding of pepper.

Potato Salad Italian Style

Serve this simple potato salad warm or at room temperature. It is also good with a splash of red wine vinegar added just before serving.

6 Servings — 171 Calories per serving

1¾ pounds small red potatoes, scrubbed
½ cup thinly sliced scallions
½ cup thinly sliced celery
¼ cup finely chopped Italian (flat leaf) parsley
3 tablespoons olive oil
¼ teaspoon salt
⅛ teaspoon freshly ground black pepper

1. Cook the potatoes in a large saucepan of boiling water until tender, 10 to 15 minutes. Drain and let cool slightly. Halve or quarter the potatoes into a serving bowl.

2. Add the scallions, celery and parsley to the potatoes. Drizzle on the olive oil. Season with the salt and pepper. Gently fold to blend. Serve at room temperature.

Plum Tomato, Red Onion and Mint Salad

A perfect salad for when tomatoes are juicy and plentiful. Serve with a platter of fresh cooked corn on the cob.

4 Servings — 139 Calories per serving

1 pound ripe plum tomatoes, quartered lengthwise, then halved crosswise into 1-inch pieces
1 medium red onion, cut into ¼-inch-thick wedges
1 small cucumber, peeled, quartered lengthwise and cut into 1-inch chunks
1 tablespoon packed chopped fresh mint or 1 teaspoon dried
1 tablespoon chopped fresh parsley

¼ teaspoon salt
3 tablespoons extra virgin olive oil
Freshly ground black pepper

1. In a serving bowl, combine the tomatoes, red onion and cucumber. Add the mint and parsley. Season with the salt.

2. Add the olive oil and toss just to blend. Season with a grinding of pepper. Serve.

Tomato, Celery and Green Olive Salad

This is a simple salad that is wonderful with grilled meat or chicken. Use the jarred, slightly crushed green olives, but rinse them well to remove as much of the salty brine as possible. Occasionally they come packed with strips of roasted red pepper; these make a nice addition to the salad.

4 Servings | 92 Calories per serving

1 pint basket cherry tomatoes
2 medium celery ribs with leafy tops
½ cup pitted green olives (see recipe introduction)
2 tablespoons olive oil
Freshly ground black pepper

1. Remove any stems from the tomatoes and cut the tomatoes lengthwise in half. Cut the leafy tops off the celery and chop enough to measure 2 tablespoons. Slice the celery ribs into ½-inch pieces.

2. In a serving bowl, combine the cherry tomatoes, sliced celery and chopped celery tops and green olives. Add the olive oil and a grinding of pepper; toss to blend. Serve at room temperature.

Tomatoes Stuffed with Orzo Salad

Kernels of raw sweet corn, always available during tomato season, add a pleasant sweetness and an interesting crunch to this salad. To save time, finely chop the harder textured vegetables, such as carrot and celery, in the food processor. Serve this salad as a first course or as a side dish with grilled seafood, beef or poultry.

8 Servings 175 Calories per serving

1 cup orzo (tiny rice-shaped pasta)
8 medium tomatoes (4 to 5 ounces each)
½ cup no-cholesterol mayonnaise
1 tablespoon fresh lemon juice
1 teaspoon red wine vinegar
½ cup packed fresh parsley sprigs
2 scallions—white bulbs coarsely chopped, green tops thinly sliced
¼ teaspoon salt
⅛ teaspoon freshly ground black pepper
½ cup fresh or thawed frozen corn kernels
½ cup finely chopped peeled carrot
½ cup finely chopped celery
½ cup finely diced green bell pepper
½ cup peeled, seeded and finely diced cucumber
Sprigs of fresh parsley and Boston lettuce leaves, for garnish

1. In a large saucepan of boiling salted water, cook the orzo until al dente, or firm to the bite, 8 to 10 minutes. Drain, rinse with cold water and let stand in the strainer until cooled to room temperature.

2. Meanwhile, core the tomatoes and cut off the tops. Coarsely chop the tops and set aside. Carefully scoop out the seeds, pulp and juice from the tomatoes, leaving sturdy shells. Invert the tomatoes on a tray lined with a double thickness of paper towel, refrigerate and let drain until ready to serve. (The tomatoes can be prepared up to 2 hours before serving.)

3. In a food processor, combine the mayonnaise, lemon juice, vinegar, parsley, coarsely chopped white part of the scallions, salt and pepper. Purée until smooth.

4. In a large bowl, combine the sliced scallion greens, corn kernels, carrot, celery, bell pepper and cucumber. Add the orzo and the mayonnaise mixture. Gently fold together with a rubber spatula until blended.

5. At serving time, spoon the orzo salad into the tomato shells. Garnish each with a sprig of parsley and serve on a lettuce leaf.

Tomato and Cucumber Salad with Oregano Vinaigrette

This salad was a family favorite when I was growing up, and it's perfect for counting calories, because there are so few. Crisp garden-fresh cucumbers are the centerpiece, surrounded by tomato wedges. The entire platter is sprinkled with a tangy red wine vinegar dressing flavored with lots of oregano. That's Italian!

4 Servings — 67 Calories per serving

3 medium cucumbers, peeled and thinly sliced on the diagonal
2 medium tomatoes, cut into thin wedges
3 tablespoons red wine vinegar
1 tablespoon olive oil
1 teaspoon minced fresh oregano or 1/4 teaspoon dried
1 garlic clove, crushed through a press
1/4 teaspoon salt
1/8 teaspoon freshly ground black pepper
Sprigs of fresh oregano or parsley, for garnish

1. In the center of a large platter, arrange the cucumber slices in concentric circles, overlapping slightly. Surround with the wedges of tomato.

2. In a small bowl, whisk together the vinegar, olive oil, oregano, garlic, salt and pepper. Drizzle evenly over the cucumbers. Garnish with sprigs of fresh oregano and serve.

— *Cannellini Bean Salad with Cherry Tomatoes* —

Beans are a healthy alternative to potatoes, rice or pasta. Here they are piquantly dressed, tossed with red onion and celery and served with cherry tomatoes, for a side salad that is pretty, tasty and sensibly controlled.

8 Servings — 153 Calories per serving

3 tablespoons extra virgin olive oil
3 tablespoons red wine vinegar
1 garlic clove, crushed through a press
¼ teaspoon salt
⅛ teaspoon freshly ground black pepper
2 cans (19 ounces each) cannellini (white kidney beans), rinsed and drained
¾ cup diced (¼ inch) red onion
½ cup finely chopped celery including a few green leaves
2 tablespoons finely chopped Italian (flat leaf) parsley
6 romaine or Boston lettuce leaves
1 cup cherry tomatoes, stems removed

1. In a large bowl, combine the olive oil, vinegar, garlic, salt and pepper. Whisk to blend. Add the cannellini beans, onion, celery and parsley; toss to blend.

2. Line a shallow bowl with the lettuce leaves; spoon the salad into the center. Garnish the salad with cherry tomatoes.

— *Fennel, Red Bell Pepper and Olive Salad* —

6 Servings — 40 Calories per serving

1 fennel bulb, about 1 pound
1 large red bell pepper
12 small brine-cured black olives, pitted and coarsely chopped
1 tablespoon extra virgin olive oil

1. Cut the dark green ends and fernlike tops off the fennel. Finely chop about 2 tablespoons of the fernlike green leaves; discard the remainder. Cut

a slice off the stem end and remove the outside ribs; discard. Cut the fennel bulb crosswise into ¼-inch-thick slices; separate into rings. Place in a bowl and add ice and water to cover. Let stand at least 1 hour.

2. Just before serving, drain the fennel and pat dry. Halve the red pepper lengthwise and remove the seeds, ribs and stem. Cut crosswise into ¼-inch-thick slices. Add to the fennel. Add the reserved chopped green fennel tops, the olives and the olive oil. Toss and serve.

Chick Pea, Tomato and Cucumber Salad

Fresh herbs are best here, but if mint or oregano is unavailable, substitute the dried variety and add them to the parsley while you are chopping it. The moisture from the parsley will help rehydrate the dried herbs.

5 Servings — 151 Calories per serving

2 tablespoons olive oil
2 tablespoons fresh lemon juice
¼ cup chopped fresh parsley
2 tablespoons chopped fresh mint or 1 teaspoon dried
2 tablespoons chopped fresh oregano or ¼ teaspoon dried
¼ teaspoon salt
⅛ teaspoon freshly ground black pepper
1 pound tomatoes (2 or 3 medium), cut into ½-inch cubes
1 medium cucumber, peeled and cut into ½-inch cubes
1 can (19 ounces) chick peas or cannellini (white kidney beans), drained and rinsed
½ cup diced (¼ inch) red onion

1. In a salad bowl, combine the olive oil, lemon juice, parsley, mint, oregano, salt and pepper. Whisk until blended.

2. Add the tomatoes, cucumber, chick peas and onion; toss to blend. Serve at room temperature.

Mozzarella and Summer Vegetable Salad

If small red and yellow pear-shaped tomatoes are available, they can be used in this salad instead of the cherry tomatoes. Use all red tomatoes, if the yellow variety are not available.

4 Servings | 164 Calories per serving

2 cups cubed (1/2 inch) zucchini (about 6 ounces)
1 pint basket cherry tomatoes (use half red and half yellow, if available), stems removed and halved
1 small cucumber, peeled and cut into 1/2-inch chunks
1 medium celery rib with leafy top, rib cut into 1/2-inch chunks, top coarsely chopped
1/2 red onion or white onion, cut into 1/2-inch cubes (about 1/2 cup)
4 ounces part-skim mozzarella cheese, cut into 3/8-inch cubes
3 tablespoons red wine vinegar
2 tablespoons olive oil
1/4 teaspoon salt, or to taste
1/8 teaspoon freshly ground black pepper
2 tablespoons coarsely chopped fresh parsley
1 tablespoon chopped fresh oregano or 1/4 teaspoon dried

1. Place a vegetable steaming rack in a large saucepan. Add 1 inch of water and bring to a boil. Add the zucchini. Cover and cook 2 minutes, or until tender. Lift the steamer from the saucepan and rinse the zucchini with cold water. Drain and let cool.

2. In a large serving bowl, combine the zucchini, tomatoes, cucumber, celery, onion and mozzarella. In a small bowl, whisk together the vinegar, olive oil, salt and pepper. Drizzle over the vegetables. Add the parsley and oregano and toss to blend.

Grilled Vegetable Salad

Grilled vegetables have an intensified, smoky flavor that is irresistible. With a minimum of calories and a maximum of taste, this sophisticated salad is guaranteed to be a hit with dieters and nondieters alike.

8 Servings — 51 Calories per serving

1 medium zucchini (about 4 ounces), halved lengthwise
1 medium red bell pepper, quartered, stem and seeds removed
1 medium yellow summer squash (about 4 ounces), halved lengthwise
1 small (5 inches) or ½ medium eggplant, halved lengthwise
1 slice of red onion, cut ½ inch thick
2 tablespoons olive oil
1 garlic clove, halved
1 teaspoon chopped fresh rosemary or ½ teaspoon dried
1 tablespoon red or white wine vinegar
Freshly ground black pepper
Sprigs of fresh rosemary, for garnish

1. On a large baking sheet, arrange the vegetables, cut sides up. In a small bowl, combine the olive oil, garlic and rosemary. Lightly brush the surfaces of all the vegetables with the seasoned oil.

2. Light a medium-hot fire in a grill. Grill the vegetables, covered, if your grill has one, 5 to 10 minutes per side, or until the vegetables are browned and tender. As the vegetables are done, transfer them to the baking sheet or a platter and let stand until cool enough to handle.

3. Cut the grilled vegetables into ¾-inch cubes. Peel off and discard any loosened pepper skins. Combine all the cubed vegetables in a large bowl. Sprinkle on the vinegar and a grinding of pepper and toss lightly. Garnish with rosemary sprigs.

Cauliflower with Herbed Bread Crumbs

Cauliflower is a crucifer, one of the family of vegetables, which includes broccoli and cabbage, that is reputed to have some effectiveness as an anti-cancer agent. It is certainly a nutritious, extremely low-calorie vegetable, and feel free to fill up on it without guilt.

4 Servings | 63 Calories per serving

1 tablespoon olive oil
½ cup coarse dry bread crumbs (preferably made from day-old Italian bread)
1 tablespoon chopped fresh parsley
1 teaspoon fresh oregano leaves or a pinch of dried
1 teaspoon fresh thyme leaves or ¼ teaspoon dried
1 garlic clove, crushed through a press
½ teaspoon grated lemon zest
⅛ teaspoon salt
Freshly ground black pepper
1 medium head of cauliflower (about 1½ pounds), broken into florets

1. Heat the olive oil in a large nonstick skillet. Add the bread crumbs and cook over medium-low heat, stirring, until golden, about 5 minutes. Add the parsley, oregano, thyme, garlic, lemon zest, salt and a grinding of pepper. Cook over low heat, stirring to blend, 1 minute. Remove from the heat and set aside.

2. Place a vegetable steaming rack in a large wide saucepan or Dutch oven. Add 1 inch of water and bring to a boil. Arrange the cauliflower on the rack. Cover and steam until the cauliflower is crisp-tender, about 10 minutes.

3. Transfer the cauliflower to a serving dish. Top with the seasoned bread crumbs and serve at once.

Chapter Five

CHICKEN AND MEAT

Low-fat, low-calorie, protein-rich chicken is as popular in Italy as it is in America. Even in the Mediterranean, it is the star meat for anyone eating light. The simplest classic Italian preparation for chicken is roasted with just a fragrant stem of rosemary tucked into the cavity. But Italian cooks prepare both chicken and turkey in a myriad of ways, cooking them whole and cut up, using every conceivable cooking technique and keeping in mind, once again, that simplicity is the operative word.

To keep the fat, cholesterol and calories to a minimum with any meat, it is important to trim off any visible clumps of external fat. This is true for chicken as well as for beef, pork or lamb. To reduce fat and calories further, remove the skin from poultry before cooking. If it is essential to insure moistness during cooking, remember to remove it before eating. A 3½-ounce portion of skinless, boneless chicken breast contains only 4 grams of fat, 75 grams of cholesterol and 150 calories. In addition, it provides half the daily USDA adult requirement of protein and is a good source of vitamin A, thiamin, riboflavin, niacin, iron, zinc, phosphorus and calcium.

Italy is not a major beef-eating country, as America is. Steak, as we know it, is a regional specialty eaten primarily in Tuscany. There magnificent cattle are raised in the hills, and traditional restaurants serve grilled slabs of beef that would make a Texan smile. Elsewhere in the country, Italians, of course, enjoy beef, veal, pork and lamb dishes, but in moderation, which makes for a leaner, healthier diet. Servings of meat are generally small because the meat course usually follows an antipasto and/or a small plate of pasta.

The following recipes lean heavily toward the Italian fondness for poultry, with just a sampling of beef, veal, lamb and pork—and a rabbit dish has been added for variety. I've tried to offer a selection of the types of preparations and authentic flavorings you would find in different regions all over Italy: Chicken Sautéed with Ham and Rosemary, Veal Stew with Lemon and Herbs, Boneless Pork Loin with Fennel Seeds, which is roasted, and Braised Beef with Currants and Orange, for example. These dishes are all light enough—400 calories maximum and many below 200—to allow plenty of room for vegetables and maybe even a serving of pasta to begin the meal or a light dessert to complete it.

Braised Chicken with Garlic and Spinach

The taste of garlic that has been slowly cooked is very unlike the harsh, pungent raw product. It becomes soft in texture with a sweet, almost toasted, nutlike flavor. Carrots and spinach make this a vitamin-packed dish that is as healthy as it is tasty.

4 SERVINGS — 278 CALORIES PER SERVING

1 chicken (3 to 3½ pounds), cut into 8 or 10 serving pieces
1 tablespoon olive oil
10 garlic cloves, peeled and halved if large
1 small carrot, peeled and halved lengthwise
½ cup unsalted or reduced-sodium chicken broth
1 pound fresh spinach, rinsed, stems trimmed, large leaves torn (about 8 cups packed)
¼ teaspoon salt
⅛ teaspoon freshly ground black pepper

1. Rinse the chicken pieces and pat dry. Remove the skin and any visible fat. Heat the olive oil in a large deep nonstick skillet or Dutch oven. Add the chicken and cook over medium heat, turning once, until lightly browned, about 5 minutes per side.

2. Add the garlic cloves and the carrot to the skillet. Cover, reduce the heat to medium-low and cook, stirring once or twice, 20 minutes. Using tongs, transfer the chicken pieces and the carrot to a serving dish; cover with aluminum foil to keep warm. Cover the skillet and cook the garlic until it is golden and soft enough to crush with a fork, about 10 minutes longer.

3. Add the chicken broth to the pan. Bring to a boil over high heat and boil until reduced by half. Transfer the broth and garlic to a food processor and purée until smooth.

4. Arrange the spinach in a layer in the skillet. Place the chicken pieces on top of the spinach. Cut the carrot crosswise into ½-inch pieces and sprinkle over the chicken. Season the chicken lightly with the salt and pepper. Pour the puréed garlic sauce over the chicken.

5. Cover and cook over medium heat just until the spinach is wilted and the chicken is heated through, about 5 minutes. Using a slotted spoon, transfer the chicken and vegetables to the serving dish. Pour the garlic sauce over the chicken and serve.

— *Chicken Braised in Spicy Fresh Tomato Sauce* —

Serve this trim, flavorful dish with a half-portion of Spaghettini with Browned Garlic (p. 64) and you'll have room for a vegetable and still come in at under 400 calories for a real Italian feast.

4 Servings — 136 Calories per serving

4 chicken thighs (1¼ pounds total), skin removed
¼ teaspoon salt
1 teaspoon olive oil
½ cup chopped onion
1 garlic clove, minced
2 cups diced trimmed ripe plum tomatoes (about 1 pound)
1 teaspoon minced fresh oregano or ¼ teaspoon dried
¼ teaspoon crushed hot red pepper, or to taste
1 tablespoon chopped fresh basil (optional)
¼ teaspoon freshly ground black pepper

1. Rinse the chicken and pat dry. Season with the salt. Heat the olive oil in a large nonstick skillet. Add the chicken and cook over medium heat, turning once, until lightly browned, about 5 minutes per side. Remove to a plate.

2. Add the onion to the skillet and cook, stirring occasionally, until tender, about 5 minutes. Add the garlic and cook 1 minute longer. Add the tomatoes, oregano and hot pepper. Bring to a boil, reduce the heat to medium-low and cook, stirring occasionally, until the sauce is thickened, about 10 minutes.

3. Return the chicken and any juices that have collected on the plate to the skillet. Cover and cook over medium heat until the chicken is cooked through with no trace of pink near the bone, about 10 minutes. Add the basil and pepper and serve.

Chicken Breasts Roasted with Lemon and Garlic

Perfectly roasted chicken perfumed with lemon and garlic is quintessential Italian eating—simple and simply delicious. To keep the chicken meat moist, roast it with the skin on; to reduce fat and calories, remove the skin before eating.

4 Servings — 278 Calories per serving

2 teaspoons olive oil
¼ teaspoon salt
Freshly ground black pepper
4 chicken breast halves (about 8 ounces each)
1 large lemon, halved
4 garlic cloves, peeled and halved

1. Preheat the oven to 400° F. In a 9 × 13-inch baking dish, combine the olive oil, salt and a grinding of pepper. Rinse off the chicken breasts and pat dry; trim off any fat. Roll the chicken in the oil mixture to coat; arrange, skin side down, in the baking dish.

2. Squeeze the juice from half the lemon over the chicken. Cut the remaining lemon half into 4 slices and place a slice of lemon and 2 garlic clove halves on each piece of chicken.

3. Bake the chicken 15 minutes. Turn the pieces over and continue baking 20 to 25 minutes longer, or until they are white to the bone, but still juicy. Serve warm or at room temperature with the pan juices spooned on top.

Chicken Sautéed with Ham and Rosemary

The aromatic fragrance and assertive flavor of rosemary is tempered here by the sweetness of the chicken and the slightly salty edge of the ham. This savory dish is so light, you have plenty of room for accompaniments of your choice.

4 Servings — 184 Calories per serving

4 chicken breast halves (about 8 ounces each), skin removed
1 teaspoon minced fresh rosemary, or ½ teaspoon dried
½ teaspoon salt
⅛ teaspoon freshly ground black pepper
1 teaspoon olive oil
2 tablespoons diced trimmed prosciutto or cured ham (about ¾ ounce)
1 celery rib, trimmed and thinly sliced
1 garlic clove, minced

1. Remove any clumps of fat from the chicken; rinse the chicken and pat dry. Season with the rosemary, salt and pepper.

2. Heat the olive oil in a large nonstick skillet. Add the chicken, meaty side down, and cook over medium heat, turning once, until lightly browned, about 5 minutes per side. Add the prosciutto, celery and garlic. Cover, reduce the heat to low and cook 20 minutes, or until the chicken is white throughout with no trace of pink near the bone, but still juicy.

Chicken Roasted with Bell Peppers

Bell peppers roasted in a very hot oven until they are blackened around the edges have a wonderful caramelized flavor. Red bell peppers are called for in the recipe, but a combination of red, green or yellow can be used, or all green if that is what is available.

4 Servings — 191 Calories per serving

2 large red bell peppers
4 large garlic cloves, peeled
1 teaspoon olive oil

4 chicken breast halves (about 8 ounces each) or 4 chicken thighs (about 6 ounces each), skin removed
1 teaspoon fresh thyme or 1/4 teaspoon dried
1/8 teaspoon salt
Freshly ground black pepper

1. Preheat the oven to 400° F. Quarter the bell peppers; remove the stems and seeds. Place the peppers and garlic cloves in a 9 × 13-inch baking dish or roasting pan. Drizzle with the olive oil; toss to coat. Bake 20 minutes, stirring once or twice.

2. Meanwhile, rinse the chicken and pat dry. Season with the thyme, salt and a grinding of pepper. Remove the baking dish from the oven. Add the chicken and stir up the peppers and garlic. Bake, turning the chicken and rearranging the peppers once or twice during the roasting time, about 45 minutes, or until the chicken is fork tender and the peppers are well done.

Boneless Pork Loin with Fennel Seeds

A well-trimmed boneless center-cut loin of pork is a lean, slender piece of meat. It cooks quickly and carves into neat round slices, which are delicious hot, at room temperature or cold in sandwiches. You can vary the flavor of this dish by using rosemary or thyme instead of the fennel seeds.

6 SERVINGS — 199 CALORIES PER SERVING

2 teaspoons fennel seeds
2 garlic cloves, crushed through a press
1/2 teaspoon salt
1/4 teaspoon freshly ground black pepper
2 pounds boneless pork loin cut from the rib end, well trimmed and tied

1. Preheat the oven to 375° F. Combine the fennel seeds, garlic, salt and pepper in a small bowl. Rub the seasonings over the entire surface of the pork.

2. Place the roast, top side up, in a small roasting pan. Roast 30 minutes; baste with the pan juices. Turn the pork over, baste and roast 30 minutes. Turn top side up, baste and roast 15 minutes. Remove from the oven and let stand 5 minutes.

3. Carefully remove the strings and carve the pork into thin slices. Spoon the pan juices over the meat.

Pork Cutlets with Green Peppers

Boneless pork cutlets, cut from the loin, are perfect for quick sautés. The hint of vinegar adds a pleasant and tangy taste to this classic combination of pork and peppers, which is excellent served with mashed potatoes or pasta.

4 Servings — 268 Calories per serving

1½ pounds boneless pork cutlets from the loin, cut ½ inch thick, all excess fat trimmed
½ teaspoon fresh thyme or ¼ teaspoon dried
⅛ teaspoon salt
⅛ teaspoon freshly ground black pepper
2 teaspoons olive oil
½ white onion, thinly sliced (about 1 cup)
3 medium green bell peppers, quartered, stems and seeds removed
1 garlic clove, crushed through a press
1 tablespoon red or white wine vinegar

1. Rub the pork cutlets with the thyme, salt and pepper. Set a large nonstick skillet over medium-high heat, add the pork cutlets and cook, turning, until lightly browned on both sides, 1 to 2 minutes per side. Transfer the meat to a dish.

2. Add the olive oil to the skillet. Add the onion and green peppers and cook over medium-high heat, stirring occasionally, until the edges begin to brown, about 5 minutes. Reduce the heat to low, add the garlic and return the pork and any juices that have collected on the plate to the skillet. Cover and cook over low heat until the peppers are wilted and the pork is cooked through, about 10 minutes.

3. Drizzle the vinegar over the pork and peppers. Add a pinch of salt to taste and a grinding of pepper.

Oregano and Lemon Marinated Lamb Spiedini

Spiedino is an Italian term used to describe foods that have been threaded on a skewer and cooked over a fire, much like shish kebab. Here cubes of lean lamb are marinated in a mixture of garlic, lemon juice and oregano and grilled or broiled. To insure even cooking, thread the meat and vegetables on separate skewers.

4 Servings — 175 Calories per serving

Juice and grated zest from 1 lemon
2 garlic cloves, crushed through a press
1 tablespoon fresh oregano or 1 teaspoon dried
¼ teaspoon coarsely ground black pepper
⅛ teaspoon salt
1 pound lean well-trimmed lamb shoulder, cut into 12 cubes, about 1½ inches square
8 cherry tomatoes, stems removed
8 medium mushrooms

1. In a medium bowl, combine the lemon juice and zest, the garlic, oregano, pepper and salt. Whisk to blend. Add the lamb and stir to coat. Cover and refrigerate at least 2 hours or overnight, stirring occasionally.

2. Light a hot fire in a grill or preheat your broiler. Thread the meat onto 3 or 4 skewers; thread the tomatoes and mushrooms on 2 separate skewers. Brush the meat and the vegetables with any marinade left in the bowl.

3. Grill or broil, turning the skewers as needed, until the meat is evenly browned, the mushrooms are golden and tender and the tomatoes are just heated through. The cooking time will vary, depending upon the heat of your grill or broiler, but allow 10 to 12 minutes for the lamb, 5 to 8 minutes for the mushrooms and about 3 minutes for the tomatoes.

4. To serve, slide the meat and vegetables off the skewers and arrange on a large platter.

Breaded Turkey Cutlet with Cucumber and Tomato Salad

Yes, they eat turkey in Italy, which makes dieting Italian style even easier. Like chicken, turkey is exceptionally low in cholesterol and other saturated fats and high in protein. Serving salad with meat is typically Italian and sensible if you're on a diet. Here the richness of the breaded turkey cutlets contrasts with the tangy salad to make a refreshing combination.

4 Servings — 380 Calories per serving

¼ cup all-purpose flour
1 cup fine dry bread crumbs
½ plus ⅛ teaspoon salt
¼ teaspoon freshly ground black pepper
2 egg whites
2 to 4 tablespoons olive oil
1 pound turkey cutlets or thinly sliced breast (about 8 pieces)
2 medium tomatoes, cut into thin wedges
½ cup peeled diced cucumber
½ red onion, cut into thin slivers
1 teaspoon red wine vinegar

1. Place the flour and bread crumbs on separate sheets of wax paper or plates. Season the flour with the ½ teaspoon salt and the pepper. Whisk the egg whites with 1 tablespoon water in a shallow soup bowl or pie plate until blended. Coat the cutlets, one at a time, first with the flour, then the egg white wash and finally the bread crumbs; gently shake off any excess coating after each addition.

2. Heat 1½ tablespoons of the olive oil in a large nonstick skillet over medium heat until hot enough to brown a crust of bread. Add the breaded cutlets in batches and cook until browned and crisp outside and tender and cooked through, 2 to 3 minutes per side. Drain on paper towels. Add up to 1½ tablespoons more oil to the pan as needed if it becomes too dry.

3. In a medium bowl, combine the tomatoes, cucumber and onion. Add 1 tablespoon olive oil, the vinegar, the remaining ⅛ teaspoon salt and a grinding of pepper; toss to blend.

4. To serve, arrange the turkey cutlets on individual plates. Top with spoonfuls of the tomato salad, distributing evenly.

Veal Stew with Lemon and Herbs

Fresh or dried rosemary or sage are both excellent additions to this simple, but richly flavored stew. Serve stew with mashed potatoes and steamed zucchini or green beans.

4 Servings — 280 Calories per serving

1 tablespoon olive oil
1 medium onion, cut into ½-inch chunks
1 tender inside celery rib with leafy top, cut into ½-inch chunks
About ¼ cup all-purpose flour
½ teaspoon salt
¼ teaspoon freshly ground black pepper
1½ pounds veal shoulder or leg, well trimmed and cut into ½-inch cubes
½ cup dry white wine
1 can (14 ounces) Italian-style plum tomatoes, with their juices
1 teaspoon minced fresh rosemary or sage or ½ teaspoon dried
½ teaspoon grated lemon zest

1. Heat 1 teaspoon of the olive oil in a large heavy nonstick skillet. Add the onion and celery, cover and cook over low heat until tender but not browned, about 8 minutes; transfer to a side dish.

2. Meanwhile, combine the flour, salt and pepper in a plastic bag. Pat the pieces of veal dry with paper towels. Add a few pieces of veal at a time to the bag; shake to coat with the seasoned flour.

3. Heat the remaining 2 teaspoons olive oil in the nonstick skillet. Add half of the veal and cook over medium heat, turning until lightly browned on all sides. Remove with a slotted spoon to the side dish with the onion and celery. Repeat with the remaining veal.

4. Add the wine to the hot skillet and bring to a boil, scraping the browned bits from the bottom of the skillet with a wooden spoon. Boil over high heat until the wine is reduced by half, about 3 minutes. Stir in the tomatoes with their juices, rosemary and lemon zest. Bring to a boil, breaking up the tomatoes with a large spoon, and boil until the sauce is slightly thickened, about 5 minutes.

5. Return the veal and vegetables and any juices that have collected in the dish to the skillet. Cover and cook over medium-low heat, stirring occasionally, until the veal is tender, about 45 minutes. Season with salt and pepper to taste.

Veal Scallopine with Mushrooms

Veal is naturally light, and mushrooms are exceptionally low in calories. Together, they create an elegant dish that will easily afford you a glass of dry white wine—only 100 calories for a 4-ounce glass.

4 Servings | 177 Calories per serving

2 tablespoons all-purpose flour
1/4 teaspoon salt
1/8 teaspoon freshly ground black pepper
4 thin veal scallops or cutlets cut from the leg (about 3/4 pound)
2 tablespoons olive oil
1 tablespoon finely chopped onion
4 large shiitake mushroom caps, stems discarded, or 4 large white mushrooms, cut into 1/4-inch slices
1 tablespoon finely chopped fresh parsley
1/4 cup dry white wine or vermouth

1. Place the flour, salt and pepper on a sheet of wax paper; mix with a fork to blend. Dredge the veal in the seasoned flour to coat lightly; set aside.

2. Heat 1 tablespoon of the olive oil in a large nonstick skillet. Add the veal and sauté over medium-high heat, turning once, until lightly browned and cooked through, about 2 minutes per side. Transfer to a serving platter and cover with aluminum foil to keep warm. Do not wipe out the skillet.

3. Add the remaining 1 tablespoon olive oil to the skillet. Add the onion and cook over medium heat until tender, about 3 minutes. Add the mushrooms and cook, stirring and turning, until lightly browned and tender, about 5 minutes. Spoon the mushrooms on top of the veal and garnish with the chopped parsley.

4. Add the wine to the skillet and boil over high heat, stirring, until reduced to 2 tablespoons, about 2 minutes. Drizzle evenly over the veal and mushrooms and serve.

Marinated Grilled Rabbit

Lean, tasty farm-raised rabbit is available fresh or frozen in many markets. Delicately flavored, much like chicken, and similarly low in fat and calories, rabbit needs to be kept moist while cooking so it does not dry out.

4 Servings | 280 Calories per serving

3 tablespoons olive oil
1 tablespoon red or white wine vinegar
1 teaspoon fresh rosemary or ½ teaspoon dried
½ teaspoon mustard
⅛ teaspoon freshly ground black pepper
1 rabbit (about 3 pounds), cut into 8 serving pieces, rinsed and patted dry

1. In a large bowl, whisk together the olive oil, vinegar, rosemary, mustard and pepper. Add the rabbit and stir to coat. Cover and refrigerate at least 2 hours or overnight, stirring occasionally.

2. Light a hot fire in a grill or preheat your broiler. Grill the rabbit or broil about 4 inches from the heat, basting frequently with the marinade left in the bowl for the first 15 to 20 minutes and turning the pieces occasionally, until the rabbit is lightly browned and the juices run clear when the meat is pierced with a fork, 20 to 25 minutes.

Beef Roast Braised in Red Wine and Tomato Sauce

Here is an Italian pot roast that anyone eating lighter will find a real treat. Serve with steamed green beans and Crostini (p. 21) to sop up all the delicious juices.

8 Servings — 225 Calories per serving

2 teaspoons olive oil
1 rump or eye round roast, about 2½ pounds, well trimmed
1 large onion, chopped
1 carrot, peeled and thinly sliced
1 celery rib, thinly sliced
1 garlic clove, bruised with side of a knife
1 bay leaf
½ cup dry red wine
1 can (14 ounces) Italian-style plum tomatoes, with their juices
1¾ cups unsalted beef stock or 1 cup canned beef broth mixed with ¾ cup water
1 tablespoon tomato paste
½ teaspoon salt
⅛ teaspoon freshly ground black pepper

1. Preheat the oven to 350° F. Heat 1 teaspoon of the olive oil in a Dutch oven. Add the beef and cook over medium-high heat, turning until browned on all sides, about 5 minutes; remove to a plate.

2. Add the remaining 1 teaspoon olive oil to the pan. Add the onion, carrot, celery, garlic and bay leaf; stir to coat with the oil. Cover, reduce the heat to low and cook, stirring occasionally, 15 minutes, or until the vegetables are very tender.

3. Add the wine to the vegetables and bring to a boil. Boil for 1 minute to reduce slightly. Stir in the tomatoes with their juices, the beef broth and tomato paste; heat to simmering.

4. Add the meat and any juices that have collected on the plate. Cover, transfer to the oven and cook 2 to 2½ hours, or until the meat is very tender when pierced with a fork.

5. Remove the meat to a platter. Ladle the liquid and solids from the Dutch oven into a food processor; purée until smooth. Return to the Dutch oven

and bring to a boil over high heat. Boil the sauce until slightly thickened, 5 to 10 minutes. Season with the salt and pepper.

6. Carve the meat into thick slices, arrange on a platter and ladle the sauce over the top.

Braised Beef with Currants and Orange

Inspired by the sweet fruit flavors often found in savory Sicilian dishes, this tasty beef dish contains dried currants or raisins and a strip of orange zest.

4 Servings — 315 Calories per serving

2 teaspoons olive oil
1½ pounds lean beef chuck, trimmed of all excess fat and cut into 2 × 1-inch chunks
½ pound fresh mushrooms, halved if large
1 large onion, cut into ½-inch chunks
1 large carrot, peeled and cut into ¼-inch-thick slices
1 garlic clove, chopped
¼ teaspoon salt
⅛ teaspoon freshly ground black pepper
1 can (14 ounces) Italian-style plum tomatoes, with their juices
2 tablespoons currants or raisins
1 strip of orange zest (2 × ½ inch)
1 bay leaf
1 tablespoon chopped fresh parsley

1. Heat the olive oil in a large wide nonaluminum saucepan or Dutch oven. Add the beef and sauté over medium-high heat, turning, until evenly browned, 5 to 7 minutes. Add the mushrooms, onion and carrot. Cook, stirring occasionally, until tender, about 5 minutes. Add the garlic and cook 1 minute longer. Season with the salt and pepper.

2. Add the tomatoes with their juices, the currants, orange zest and bay leaf. Bring to a boil, breaking up the tomatoes with a large spoon. Reduce the heat to low, cover and cook 2 hours, or until the meat is very tender.

3. Uncover and boil gently until the sauce is slightly thickened. Season with salt and pepper to taste. Remove the bay leaf and garnish with chopped parsley before serving.

Chapter Six

SEAFOOD

The healthy Italian diet includes as much seafood as red meat and poultry. This comes as no surprise when you consider that Italy is a peninsula jutting into the Mediterranean Sea and is surrounded by smaller seas on three sides. The varieties of seafood found in these waters are richly varied, and Italian cooks take good advantage of the bounty. While many of the marine delicacies of the Italian table are highly regional—the tiny, sweet two-necked clams found off the coast of Liguria, which are steamed with white wine, olive oil and garlic and tossed with pasta, and the mild but richly flavored San Pietro of the Mediterranean—I've translated many of these authentic recipes into dishes made with seafood commonly found in fish markets all over the United States.

Fish is an excellent dietary choice for the calorie-conscious person because it is very high in protein, lower than red meat in saturated fat and a good source of a number of valuable minerals and trace elements, such as iodine, zinc and phosphorus. Shrimp and other shellfish do contain a fair amount of cholesterol, but they are very low in total saturated fat and are a good source of Omega-3 fatty acids, which many nutritionists believe actually help to lower cholesterol levels.

Inspired by the Italian flair for subtle seasonings that highlight the flavor and freshness of the seafood, rather than rich, high-fat sauces that mask the natural taste, the following recipes use very basic ingredients and are as appealing for their good taste and lean content as they are for their simplicity and ease in preparation. Citrus juices, herbs, a drizzle of olive oil, capers and olives, and perhaps a little chopped tomato, onion and garlic—all packed with flavor and generally low in fat—are the main ingredients of Italian seafood cooking.

All of the recipes and portions in this chapter are designed as main-course servings. They are so low in calories, though—most under 300—that they leave plenty of room for rice or pasta and a vegetable. Keep in mind that many of these dishes, served in smaller portions, would also be quite appropriate served elsewhere in a meal. Passed on a tray, Clams Oreganata and Marinated Grilled Shrimp, as examples, would make popular hot hors d'oeuvres. At a multicourse dinner party, Clams in Fresh Tomato Sauce or Mussels in White Wine would be a superb first course. And a smaller portion of any of the seafood salads at the end of this chapter would make a fine addition to any antipasto platter.

Sea Bass Baked with Onion, Olives and Oregano

This delicate white fish pairs beautifully with savory seasonings to produce a dish that is as light as it is flavorful.

4 Servings — 283 Calories per serving

1 tablespoon extra virgin olive oil
1 white onion, thinly sliced (about 1¼ cups)
1 tablespoon fresh oregano or ½ teaspoon dried
2 tablespoons coarsely chopped pitted black olives (Gaeta or Kalamata)
2 pounds (about 4 pieces) sea bass fillets or 2 large grouper or red snapper fillets, cut in half
1 tablespoon fresh lemon juice
⅛ teaspoon freshly ground black pepper
Thick lemon slices and sprigs of fresh oregano or parsley, for garnish

1. Preheat the oven to 350° F. Combine the olive oil, onion and half of the oregano in a 9 × 13-inch baking dish; stir to blend. Bake, stirring occasionally, 25 minutes, or until the onion is tender and beginning to brown about the edges. Stir in the olives.

2. Arrange the fish fillets on the onion mixture. Season the fish with the remaining oregano, the lemon juice and pepper. Bake 10 minutes, or until the fish is cooked through and opaque in the center, but still moist.

3. Garnish with lemon slices and sprigs of oregano. Season generously with pepper.

Fish Fillets Roasted with Sliced Potatoes and Thyme

Fish baked with potatoes is an Italian classic, but it is traditionally bathed in olive oil. Here I've turned it into a satisfying yet light dish without sacrificing taste by roasting the potatoes first, until they're lightly browned, marinating the fish for extra flavor and combining the two at the end to finish the cooking. Serve with a side dish of broccoli or green beans.

4 Servings — 356 Calories per serving

4 red snapper, sea bass or other firm white fish fillets (about 6 ounces each)
1 tablespoon fresh lemon juice
1 garlic clove, thinly sliced
1/4 teaspoon dried thyme
4 cups thinly sliced peeled all-purpose potatoes (about 1 1/2 pounds)
2 tablespoons olive oil
1/4 teaspoon salt
1/4 teaspoon freshly ground black pepper

1. Preheat the oven to 400° F. Place the fish fillets on a plate; sprinkle with the lemon juice, half the garlic and half the thyme. Cover and refrigerate until ready to bake.

2. Spread the potatoes in a 9 × 13-inch baking dish. Sprinkle the olive oil, the remaining garlic and thyme over the potato slices. Season with half the salt and pepper; toss to coat. Bake, turning with a wide spatula once or twice, until the edges of the potato slices are golden, about 35 minutes.

3. Place the fish fillets directly on top of the potatoes. Season with the remaining salt and pepper. Bake just until the fillets are opaque to the center, 5 to 8 minutes. Serve at once.

Cod Baked with Tomatoes and Capers

Fresh cod is mild in flavor, and some studies have indicated that the oil in fish may help lower bad cholesterol in the blood. Serve this zesty baked fish with crusty Roasted Potatoes with Garlic and Rosemary (p. 94).

4 SERVINGS — 164 CALORIES PER SERVING

1 teaspoon olive oil
1 cup thinly sliced onion (1 medium)
1 garlic clove, thinly sliced
1 strip of orange zest (1½ × ½ inch)
1 teaspoon fresh rosemary or ½ teaspoon dried
1 can (14 ounces) Italian-style plum tomatoes, with their juices
1 teaspoon capers, rinsed well
1¼ pounds cod fillets or 1½ pounds cod steaks, cut into 4 serving pieces
1 tablespoon fresh orange juice
Freshly ground black pepper

1. Preheat the oven to 400° F. Combine the olive oil, onion, garlic, orange zest and half of the rosemary in a 9 × 13-inch baking dish; stir to blend. Bake, stirring once, 10 minutes, or until the onion begins to brown.

2. Add the tomatoes with their juices, breaking up the tomatoes with the side of a large spoon. Add the capers. Bake, stirring occasionally, 15 minutes, or until the tomatoes begin to thicken.

3. Remove the pan from the oven; leave the oven on. Arrange the cod fillets on the tomato sauce. Sprinkle the remaining rosemary, the orange juice and a generous grinding of pepper over the fish. Spoon the tomato sauce from the pan up over the cod.

4. Return to the oven and bake 10 to 12 minutes, or until the fish is opaque to the center when it is tested with the tip of a knife.

Swordfish with Tomatoes and Fennel

The delicate, aniselike taste of fennel combined with both lemon and orange zest adds a distinctly Mediterranean note to this tomato sauce. Swordfish is excellent here, but feel free to substitute salmon, halibut, cod or bluefish.

4 Servings — 303 Calories per serving

2 teaspoons olive oil
1 small fennel bulb, trimmed, quartered and cut into thin slices crosswise
½ cup chopped onion
1 garlic clove, crushed through a press
1 can (14 ounces) Italian-style plum tomatoes, with their juices
3 strips of lemon zest (2 × ½ inch each)
1 strip of orange zest (about 3 × ½ inch)
½ teaspoon dried fennel seeds
1½ pounds swordfish steak, ½ inch thick, cut into 4 pieces
⅛ teaspoon salt
Freshly ground black pepper

1. In a large flameproof baking dish or gratin dish, heat the olive oil over medium-low heat. Add the fennel and onion and cook, stirring occasionally, until tender, about 10 minutes; do not brown. Stir in the garlic.

2. Add the tomatoes with their juices, the strips of lemon and orange zest and the fennel seeds. Bring to a boil, reduce the heat to low and simmer, breaking up the tomatoes with the side of a large spoon, until the sauce is slightly thickened, about 10 minutes.

3. Preheat your broiler. Arrange the fish in the baking dish, pushing the tomato sauce to the sides. Broil about 3 inches from the heat 5 to 8 minutes, or until the fish is opaque to the center. Season the fish with the salt and a generous grinding of pepper. Serve at once and spoon some of the sauce over each piece of fish.

— *Broiled Swordfish with Lemon and Rosemary* —

This basic marinade of lemon, olive oil, black pepper and rosemary is a classic combination that goes especially well with swordfish. It is a wonderful light summer dish that I like to serve with a tomato salad.

4 Servings — 234 Calories per serving

1 lemon
2 tablespoons olive oil
1 garlic clove, crushed through a press
1 tablespoon fresh rosemary or 1 teaspoon dried
1¼ pounds swordfish, about 1 inch thick, cut into 4 pieces
Freshly ground black pepper
Sprigs of fresh rosemary or parsley, for garnish

1. Using a hand grater, grate or finely shred the zest (yellow skin) from the lemon. Halve the lemon and squeeze the juice from one half. Combine the lemon zest, lemon juice, olive oil, garlic and rosemary in a large shallow dish. Cut the remaining lemon half into 4 thin slices and set aside for garnish.

2. Add the fish to the marinade and turn to coat. Cover and refrigerate up to 2 hours, basting occasionally.

3. Light a hot fire in a grill or preheat your broiler. Grill or broil the swordfish, basting once or twice with the marinade, until browned on the bottom, about 5 minutes. Baste again, turn the fish over and cook until the other side is browned and the swordfish is opaque to the center, about 5 to 8 minutes. Season with a grinding of pepper and garnish with the lemon slices and sprigs of rosemary.

Shellfish with Chopped Fresh Tomatoes and Garlic Croutons

Shellfish are exceedingly low in calories, and for most people they are a real treat, which makes this is a wonderful party dish. Use all clams, all mussels or a mixture of both, as suggested below.

4 Servings | 209 Calories per serving

1 cup dry white wine
½ cup diced red onion
¼ cup coarsely chopped Italian (flat leaf) parsley
1 teaspoon fresh thyme or ¼ teaspoon dried
1 strip of orange zest (1½ × ½ inch), finely chopped
1¼ pounds juicy ripe plum tomatoes, cored and coarsely chopped (about 3 cups)
Freshly ground black pepper
12 littleneck clams, scrubbed
12 mussels, scrubbed and debearded
4 large shrimp (about 8 ounces), shelled and deveined
Garlic Croutons (recipe follows)

1. In a large wide nonaluminum saucepan or Dutch oven, bring the white wine to a boil. Add the red onion, parsley, thyme and orange zest and boil over high heat 2 minutes. Add the tomatoes and bring to a boil, stirring often. Add a generous grinding of pepper.

2. Place the clams and mussels in a layer on the bottom of the pan; arrange the shrimp on top. Cover and cook over high heat 5 minutes, or until the mussels and clams are opened and the shrimp are cooked through and opaque throughout.

3. Using a slotted spoon, transfer the shellfish to a large deep platter. Discard any clams or mussels that do not open. Scoop out any vegetables from the broth and add to the shellfish. Ladle the broth over the shellfish, leaving behind any grit at the bottom of the pan.

4. Crumble the Garlic Croutons coarsely with your fingers. Sprinkle the crumbs over the shellfish and serve at once.

Garlic Croutons

Makes about 1 cup, 16 tablespoons — 52 Calories per tablespoon

½ garlic clove
4 slices of Italian bread, cut ½ inch thick
1 tablespoon olive oil
Salt and freshly ground black pepper

1. Preheat the oven to 350° F. Rub the cut side of the garlic over one side of each bread slice. Using a pastry brush, lightly coat both sides of the bread with the olive oil. Cut the bread into ½-inch cubes.

2. Place the bread cubes on a baking sheet and bake, turning once or twice, until the croutons are golden, about 20 minutes. Season lightly with salt and pepper.

Clams in Fresh Tomato Sauce

4 Servings — 160 Calories per serving

1 tablespoon olive oil
½ cup chopped white onion
2 garlic cloves, finely chopped
2 pounds ripe juicy tomatoes, cored and chopped (about 4½ cups)
4 dozen littleneck clams, scrubbed and rinsed
¼ cup chopped fresh basil or Italian (flat leaf) parsley

1. Heat the olive oil in a large deep nonaluminum skillet or Dutch oven. Add the onion and cook over medium heat, stirring, until tender, about 5 minutes. Add the garlic and cook 1 minute longer. Add the tomatoes and bring to a boil. Cook, stirring occasionally, 10 minutes.

2. Add the clams, cover and raise the heat to high. Cook until the clams are opened, about 5 minutes. With a slotted spoon, remove the clams to a large shallow serving bowl. Discard any clams that do not open. Boil the tomato sauce, stirring often, until slightly reduced, about 5 minutes. Stir the basil into the sauce and pour over the clams.

Clams Oreganata

Ask your fish purveyor to open the clams and leave them on the half shell. Or open them yourself: First spread the clams in a baking pan and place in the freezer for about 1 hour. The freezing temperature causes the muscles to relax, making the clams easier to open.

4 Servings — 112 Calories per serving

2 to 3 cups rock salt
24 small cherrystone or 12 large littleneck clams, scrubbed and opened but left on the half shell
1 tablespoon olive oil
1 cup coarse dry bread crumbs (preferably made from day-old Italian bread)
2 tablespoons finely chopped Italian (flat leaf) parsley
2 teaspoons minced fresh oregano or ½ teaspoon dried
1 garlic clove, crushed through a press
1 strip of bacon, cooked until crisp, drained and crumbled
Freshly ground black pepper

1. Preheat the oven to 400° F. Spread the rock salt in a 9 × 13-inch baking pan. Arrange the shucked clams in rows on the rock salt.

2. Add the olive oil to a large nonstick skillet and tilt to coat the bottom evenly. Sprinkle with the bread crumbs. Turn heat to medium-low and heat the crumbs, stirring frequently, until they begin to turn golden, about 8 minutes. Add the parsley, oregano, garlic and bacon. Cook, stirring, 1 minute. Season with a generous grinding of pepper.

3. Using a teaspoon, sprinkle a thick layer of the crumb mixture on top of each clam. Bake 10 to 12 minutes, or until the crumbs are golden. Serve at once.

Mussels in White Wine

Steamed mussels can be served as a satisfying first course or main course on their own, ladled hot over a platter of linguine or with crostini to soak up the fragrant juices. They are also good served cold or at room temperature. Look for farm-raised mussels in your supermarket or fish store; they tend to be more uniform in size, cleaner and of a more consistent quality.

4 Servings — 135 Calories per serving

2 pounds mussels
1 tablespoon olive oil
1 small onion, sliced
1 garlic clove, bruised with side of a knife
1 strip of orange zest (2 × ½ inch)
1 cup dry white wine
1 sprig of Italian (flat leaf) parsley and/or fresh basil
½ red onion, cut into thin rings, for garnish
2 tablespoons chopped fresh Italian (flat leaf) parsley, for garnish

1. Shortly before cooking, tap any slightly opened mussels with a finger until they begin to close. Discard any mussels with cracked shells or that refuse to close. Pull off the hairy brown threads, called beards, with your fingers or cut them off with a small, sharp knife. Rinse the shells, thoroughly rubbing any rough spots with a coarse brush. Soak in very cold fresh tap water 5 minutes before cooking.

2. Heat the olive oil in a large deep skillet or Dutch oven. Add the onion and cook over medium heat, stirring occasionally, until tender, about 5 minutes. Add the garlic and orange zest and cook 1 minute. Add the wine and herb sprig and bring to a boil.

3. Drain the mussels and add them to the boiling wine. Cover and cook over high heat 4 to 5 minutes, or until all the mussels are opened. Using a slotted spoon, transfer the mussels to a large platter and cover with aluminum foil to keep warm. Discard any mussels that do not open. Carefully strain the liquid through a fine sieve set over a 2-cup glass measure. Discard the solids. Return the liquid to the skillet and reheat.

4. Pour the hot liquid over the mussels. Garnish with red onion rings and chopped parsley.

Mussels in Spicy Tomato Sauce

Serve this tasty dish with crusty bread to mop up the juices—55 calories for 2 slices of Italian bread cut ½ inch thick—or boil the juices until thickened and pour over 3 ounces of cooked pasta for roughly 210 calories.

4 Servings — 133 Calories per serving

1 tablespoon olive oil
¼ cup chopped onion
2 garlic cloves, finely chopped
1 can (28 ounces) Italian-style plum tomatoes, with their juices
1 strip of orange zest (2 × ½ inch)
1 sprig of fresh basil or a pinch of dried
1 teaspoon fresh oregano or ¼ teaspoon dried
Pinch of crushed hot red pepper
2 pounds mussels

1. Heat the olive oil in a large deep nonaluminum skillet or Dutch oven. Add the onion and cook over medium heat until tender, 3 to 5 minutes. Add the garlic and cook 1 minute longer. Add the tomatoes with their juices, orange zest, basil, oregano and hot pepper. Bring to a boil. Reduce the heat to medium-low and simmer 10 minutes.

2. Meanwhile, sort the mussels, tapping any slightly opened shells with a finger until they begin to close. Discard any mussels with cracked shells or that refuse to close. Pull off the hairy brown threads, called beards, with your fingers or cut them off with a small, sharp knife. Rinse the shells, thoroughly rubbing any rough spots with a coarse brush. Soak in very cold fresh tap water for 5 minutes before cooking.

3. Drain the mussels and add them to the simmering tomato sauce. Cover and cook over high heat until the mussels have opened, about 5 minutes.

4. With a slotted spoon, remove the mussels to a serving platter. Discard any that do not open. Boil the sauce, uncovered, over high heat, stirring often, until thickened. Spoon the sauce over the mussels and serve at once.

Marinated Grilled Shrimp

Shrimp are especially flavorful grilled outdoors, but when that's not possible, searing the shrimp over high heat in a nonstick skillet yields very good results, too. The outside becomes crunchy with the spices and the interior stays sweet and juicy.

4 Servings | 131 Calories per serving

1 tablespoon olive oil
2 garlic cloves, crushed through a press
1 teaspoon grated orange zest
½ teaspoon crushed hot red pepper
½ teaspoon dried thyme
24 large shrimp (about 1 pound), shelled but with tails left on and deveined

1. Combine the olive oil, garlic, orange zest, hot pepper and thyme on a platter or pie plate; stir to blend. Add the shrimp and press the marinade on with your fingertips. Cover and refrigerate at least 2 hours or up to 8 hours before cooking.

2. To grill the shrimp, light a hot fire in a grill. Thread the shrimp onto skewers, spearing them through both ends to hold them securely. Grill, turning once, until browned outside and opaque throughout, about 2 minutes per side.

NOTE *To cook the shrimp in a skillet, heat a large nonstick skillet over high heat until hot enough to evaporate a drop of water upon contact. Add the shrimp, a few at a time, so the skillet doesn't cool down and cook, turning once, until browned and crusty outside and opaque to the center, about 2 minutes per side.*

Shrimp with White Wine and Tomatoes

Very simple, very pretty and very lean, this elegant dish could star at any dinner party. Serve with steamed spinach, and you'll have plenty of calories left over for a small serving of pasta or rice and even a light dessert.

4 Servings — 135 Calories per serving

1 tablespoon olive oil
2 cloves garlic, crushed through a press
½ cup dry white wine
16 extra-large shrimp (about 1 pound), shelled but with tails left on and deveined
½ cup drained, peeled and coarsely chopped fresh or canned plum tomatoes
⅛ teaspoon salt
⅛ teaspoon freshly ground black pepper
1½ tablespoons finely chopped Italian (flat leaf) parsley

1. Heat the olive oil in a large nonstick skillet over low heat. Add the garlic and cook, stirring, until it is fragrant, about 2 minutes.

2. Add the wine. Raise the heat to high and boil until reduced by half, 3 to 5 minutes. Add the shrimp and tomatoes and cook over medium heat, stirring often, until the shrimp are just cooked through and opaque throughout, 2 to 3 minutes. Season with the salt and pepper and garnish with chopped parsley.

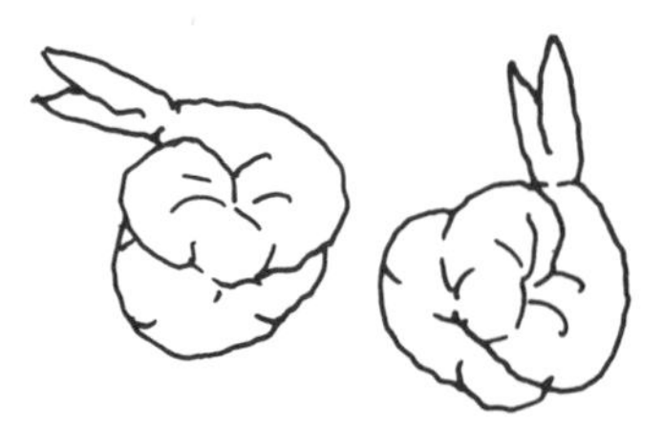

Calamari in Red Sauce

When I was growing up, my mother's calamari in red sauce was our standard Friday night supper. I still remember watching with fascination as my mother carefully cleaned those monstrous-looking sea creatures, also known as squid. Today, we're lucky, because it is not unusual to find the squid already cleaned and ready to cook. It is best to use squid the same day it is purchased. If you are using frozen cleaned squid, defrost in a bowl of cold water, changing the water often while defrosting.

4 Servings — 207 Calories per serving

1½ pounds cleaned medium squid
2 tablespoons olive oil
4 garlic cloves, halved
½ teaspoon crushed hot red pepper
1 can (14 ounces) Italian-style plum tomatoes, with their juices
¼ cup chopped Italian (flat leaf) parsley
Freshly ground black pepper

1. Rinse the squid inside and out under cold running water; drain well. Cut the bodies crosswise into ½-inch circles; leave the tentacles whole. Pat the squid dry between paper towels.

2. In a large heavy skillet, combine the olive oil and garlic. Cook over medium-low heat until the garlic is lightly browned, about 5 minutes. Discard the garlic.

3. Add the hot pepper to the oil, raise the heat to medium and cook 1 minute. Add the squid, a few at a time, and cook, stirring often, until the liquid evaporates and the squid begin to brown, 3 to 5 minutes.

4. Add the tomatoes with their juices and the parsley. Bring to a simmer, breaking up the tomatoes with the side of a large spoon. Cover, reduce the heat to low and cook, stirring occasionally, until the squid are very tender, about 30 minutes. Before serving, season with a grinding of pepper.

Shrimp and White Bean Salad

Both shrimp and white beans are high in protein and low in fat. Together they make a light but sophisticated pairing that can be served for lunch or as a cool supper.

4 Servings | 248 Calories per serving

3 tablespoons olive oil
2 tablespoons red wine vinegar
½ garlic clove, crushed through a press
¼ teaspoon salt
⅛ teaspoon freshly ground black pepper
1 can (19 ounces) cannellini (white kidney beans), rinsed and drained
8 ounces medium shrimp, shelled, deveined and cooked
½ cup diced (¼ inch) celery
½ cup sliced scallions
2 tablespoons finely chopped Italian (flat leaf) parsley
Romaine lettuce leaves
1 cup diced (½ inch) plum tomatoes

1. In a large bowl, combine the olive oil, vinegar, garlic, salt and pepper. Whisk until blended. Add the beans, shrimp, celery, scallions and parsley. Toss gently to coat with the dressing.

2. Line a platter with the lettuce leaves and spoon the salad into the center. Garnish with the diced tomatoes.

Shrimp and Celery Salad

The crisp, cool celery is a pleasant contrast to the soft texture and briny flavor of the shrimp in this appealing salad. Only ½ tablespoon of extra virgin olive oil per person adds wonderful flavor without a lot of calories or fat.

4 Servings | 175 Calories per serving

2 large outer celery ribs plus 3 to 4 leafy tops
½ small yellow onion
1 bay leaf
1 pound large shrimp, shelled and deveined
½ garlic clove
½ cup thinly sliced red onion
¼ cup coarsely chopped Italian (flat leaf) parsley
2 tablespoons fresh lemon juice
Radicchio or red-tipped lettuce leaves
2 tablespoons extra virgin olive oil
Freshly ground black pepper
Lemon wedges, for garnish

1. Cut the celery ribs into ¼-inch slices. Set 1 leafy top aside. Coarsely chop enough of the remaining celery leaves to measure ¼ cup.

2. Fill a large saucepan with water. Add the whole celery top, onion half and bay leaf. Bring to a boil, reduce the heat, cover and simmer 5 minutes. Add the shrimp and bring to a boil, stirring often. Boil 3 minutes, or until the shrimp are pink, loosely curled and opaque throughout. Drain and rinse under cold running water until cool; drain well. Cover and refrigerate until chilled, at least 30 minutes.

3. Rub the inside of a large salad bowl with the cut side of the garlic. Add the chilled shrimp, sliced celery ribs, chopped celery leaves, red onion and parsley to the bowl. Drizzle the lemon juice over the salad and toss to blend.

4. Line a large shallow bowl or platter with the radicchio leaves; spoon the shrimp salad into the center. Drizzle the olive oil over the salad and season with a generous grinding of pepper. Garnish with lemon wedges.

Mussel and Potato Salad

This hearty salad makes a satisfying main dish. Serve with a cold glass of crisp white wine from Tuscany—only 100 calories for 4 ounces.

4 Servings | 218 Calories per serving

1 pound medium red potatoes
2 dozen mussels
1 large celery rib with leafy top plus 2 tablespoons minced leafy celery top
1 onion slice
1 bay leaf
1 garlic clove, bruised with side of a knife
½ cup diced red onion
½ cup fresh cooked or thawed frozen green peas
2 tablespoons diced roasted red pepper
2 tablespoons minced Italian (flat leaf) parsley
2 tablespoons fresh lemon juice
2 tablespoons olive oil
Freshly ground black pepper
Lettuce leaves and tomato wedges, for garnish

1. Cook the potatoes in a large saucepan of boiling water until tender to the center, 20 to 25 minutes. Drain and let stand until cool enough to handle. Peel off the skins and cut the potatoes into ½-inch cubes; set aside.

2. Sort the mussels by tapping any slightly opened shells with a finger until they begin to close. Discard any mussels with cracked shells or that refuse to close. Pull off the hairy brown threads, called beards, with your fingers or cut them off with a small, sharp knife. Rinse the shells, thoroughly rubbing any rough spots with a coarse brush. Soak in very cold fresh tap water 5 minutes before cooking.

3. Cut the top off the large celery rib. Dice the celery and set aside. Place the leafy top in a large wide saucepan or Dutch oven. Add ½ cup of water, the onion slice, bay leaf and garlic. Bring to a boil, reduce the heat and simmer 5 minutes. Raise the heat to high. Add the mussels, cover and cook until the mussels open, 3 to 5 minutes. With a slotted spoon, remove the mussels from the broth. Ladle out ¼ cup of the broth and reserve. Let the mussels cool; then remove them from the shells.

4. In a large bowl, combine the potatoes and the ¼ cup reserved mussel broth; toss to coat. Add the mussels, diced and minced celery, diced red onion, peas, roasted red pepper, parsley, lemon juice, olive oil and a generous grinding of pepper. Toss to blend. Serve on a platter lined with lettuce leaves; garnish with tomato wedges. Serve cold or at room temperature.

Calamari, Basil and Tomato Salad

Calamari, squid, should be cooked quickly in boiling water—less than 1 minute—or simmered slowly for 20 to 30 minutes. Anything in between and you will find the squid to be more like rubber bands than its sweet, tender self. For the following salad look for small calamari and use the quick-cooking method.

4 Servings — 205 Calories per serving

1 pound cleaned small squid
½ teaspoon salt
2 cups diced (½ inch) plum tomatoes
1 cup sliced (½ inch) celery
1 cup diced (½ inch) sweet yellow onion
¼ cup packed chopped fresh basil or Italian (flat leaf) parsley
2 tablespoons extra virgin olive oil
¼ teaspoon salt
⅛ teaspoon freshly ground black pepper
Lime wedges, for garnish

1. Rinse the squid inside and out under cold running water; drain well. Cut the bodies crosswise into ½-inch rings; cut the tentacles in half. Pat dry between paper towels.

2. In a large saucepan, bring 2 quarts of water to a boil; add the salt. Add the squid and cook over high heat, stirring constantly, for 45 seconds, or until the squid turns opaque. Drain at once into a colander and rinse under cold running water, tossing the squid until they are cooled; drain well.

3. In a serving bowl, combine the squid with the tomatoes, celery, onion, basil, olive oil, salt and pepper. Toss to blend. Garnish with lime wedges.

Tuna, Fennel and Red Pepper Salad

Imported and domestic brands of tuna packed in olive oil are juicy and flavorful, and the tuna oil can be used to dress the salad. Lots of color, texture and volume are added here by an appetizing selection of vegetables. For a change of pace, use chopped fennel instead of celery to add crunch and texture, and red bell pepper instead of green pepper for sweetness and color. Remember to grate the zest from the lemon before extracting the juice.

4 Servings — 300 Calories per serving

2 tablespoons fresh lemon juice
½ garlic clove, crushed through a press
2 cans (6½ ounces each) tuna packed in olive oil, oil reserved
2 tablespoons finely chopped Italian (flat leaf) parsley
1 teaspoon grated lemon zest
Coarsely ground black pepper
½ cup chopped trimmed fennel or celery
½ cup chopped red or yellow bell pepper
½ cup chopped red onion
Romaine or other lettuce leaves
8 slices (¼ inch) peeled cucumber
4 whole radishes
4 whole scallions
4 brine-cured black olives, such as Kalamata
4 lemon wedges

1. In a medium bowl, whisk together the lemon juice and garlic. Add the tuna with its oil, the parsley, lemon zest and a generous grinding of pepper. Toss gently with a fork to mix.

2. In a separate bowl, combine the fennel, bell pepper and red onion; toss to blend. Add to the tuna and stir once or twice just to blend.

3. Line a platter with the lettuce leaves. Spoon the tuna salad onto the leaves. Garnish with the cucumber slices, radishes, scallions, black olives and lemon wedges.

Chapter Seven

PIZZA AND PANINI

Although pizza is Italian in origin, there's no question that it is an all-American staple. Like pasta, pizza has been mistakenly maligned as heavy and fattening. In fact, pizza can be a highly nutritious dish, especially if the saturated fat is kept under control.

I think you'll be pleasantly surprised at the substantial amounts you can eat of the pizzas that follow and still maintain a healthy diet. The crusts are hearty and chewy. To keep them light, I've cut back on the quantity of the cheese, but that's more than compensated for by the addition of plenty of lean, good-tasting and nutritious fresh vegetables. Topped with pieces of broccoli, slices of tomato, mushroom or onion, wedges of sweet bell peppers and a sprinkling of herbs, these tempting pizzas offer an exceptionally satisfying supper—all low in fat and containing 400 calories or less per serving.

Mozzarella, the popular pizza cheese that melts so beautifully, is now available in four different nutritional forms: whole milk, part-skim, reduced-fat and fat-free. The chart on page 154 compares the calories and grams of fat per ounce for each type. The reduced-fat and fat-free mozzarellas do not have the familiar stretchy consistency and soft texture of the whole milk and part-skim mozzarellas. They do, however, allow a freedom of choice in diet never before possible in terms of fat and calories. The higher fat mozzarellas will add 40 to 50 calories to the recipes that follow; if you choose to use them, remember to compensate elsewhere in your daily diet.

Once the pizza dough is prepared, adding the toppings and baking the pizza takes less than half an hour. The following pizza recipes have been created to make 4 individual pizza servings or one large 15-inch pizza that can be shared by 4.

Focaccia is a thick flat bread made with the same dough as pizza, but topped in a much simpler fashion. Here it is suggested as an accompaniment or side dish. I often serve a basket of focaccia cut into small squares as a snack with a glass of wine before dinner.

Panino actually means bread or roll. In train stations throughout Italy and in espresso cafes all over the country, vendors sell *panini*—small, light, often open-faced sandwiches, or small crusty rolls filled with slices of cheese, vegetables or meat—as snacks. The assortment here includes lean vegetables and a chicken filling, instead of meat, combined to pique your appetite. If you can buy real rectangular Italian rolls, by all means use them instead of the bread suggested in the recipes. The sandwiches are also delicious when served on thick slices of sourdough or other coarse, chewy peasant-style bread.

A Guide to Mozzarella Cheeses

FAT-FREE MOZZARELLA	40 calories	0gm. fat per ounce
REDUCED-FAT MOZZARELLA	60 calories	3gm. fat per ounce
PART-SKIM MOZZARELLA	80 calories	5gm. fat per ounce
WHOLE MILK MOZZARELLA	80 calories	6gm. fat per ounce

Pizza Dough

This recipe is for both a plain pizza dough and a part whole wheat pizza dough. Although whole wheat pizza is slightly unorthodox, the small amount of whole wheat flavor gives the crust a pleasant chewy texture and nutty flavor, and it's actually slightly lower in calories than pizza made with all-purpose white flour. Note that both pizzas call for *unbleached* all-purpose flour.

Pizza dough can be made very easily in a heavy-duty mixer, food processor or by hand. The following recipe first gives directions for making the dough with a heavy-duty mixer. Directions for making pizza in a food processor and by hand are also detailed below.

Makes enough dough for one 15-inch pizza to serve 4, or four 7-inch pizzas

1 cup lukewarm water (105° F. to 115° F.)
1 envelope (1/4 ounce) active dry yeast

Whole Wheat Flour Dough: 285 Calories per serving

1 tablespoon olive oil
1½ to 2 cups unbleached all-purpose flour or bread flour
½ cup whole wheat flour
½ teaspoon salt

All-Purpose Flour Dough: 291 Calories per serving

1 tablespoon olive oil
2 to 2½ cups unbleached all-purpose flour
½ teaspoon salt

1. In a large bowl, combine the warm water and the yeast. Cover with plastic wrap and let stand until the yeast is dissolved, about 5 minutes.

2. *Whole wheat flour dough:* Stir in the olive oil, 1½ cups of the all-purpose flour, the whole wheat flour and the salt until blended.

3. *All-purpose flour dough:* Stir in the olive oil, 2 cups of the all-purpose flour and the salt until blended.

4. If using an electric mixer, use the paddle attachment and gradually beat in as much of the remaining ½ cup all-purpose flour as needed to make a smooth dough that pulls together and freely cleans the sides of the bowl.

5. Remove the paddle attachment and insert the dough hook. Knead the dough 5 minutes. Transfer to a lightly floured board and knead with your hands just until the dough is smooth to the touch and springs back when lightly poked with a fingertip.

6. Shape the dough into a smooth ball, place in a large bowl, cover with plastic wrap and let stand in warm place until doubled in volume, 1 to 1½ hours.

Food processor method: In a small bowl, dissolve the yeast as directed in step 1 above. Combine half of the flour and the salt in the food processor; pulse just to blend. Add the olive oil to the yeast and water mixture. With the machine on, add the liquid ingredients all at once; process until a dough forms. Gradually add small amounts of the remaining flour, pulsing briefly after each addition, until a soft smooth dough forms. Scrape the dough out onto a lightly floured surface. Knead in as much of the remaining flour as needed by hand to form a smooth but moist, not dry, dough. Let rise as directed above.

Hand method: Dissolve the yeast in the water in a large bowl. Add half of the flour, the olive oil and salt; stir until blended. Gradually stir in the remaining flour until the mixture forms a ball that cleans the sides of the bowl. Turn out onto a lightly floured surface and knead 8 to 10 minutes, adding as much of the remaining flour as needed to form a smooth dough that springs back when poked with a fingertip. Let rise as directed above.

NOTE *For portion control all the pizza recipes that follow make 4 individual pizzas. If you prefer, 1 large pizza can be made, either round, 15 inches in diameter, or rectangular, 15 × 10 inches.*

— Red Onion, Bell Pepper and Rosemary Pizza —

4 Servings | 393 Calories per serving

4 cups thinly sliced red onions
2 teaspoons olive oil
1 medium red bell pepper, cut into thin 2-inch slivers
1 teaspoon minced fresh rosemary or ½ teaspoon dried
⅛ teaspoon salt
⅛ teaspoon freshly ground black pepper
1 recipe Pizza Dough (p. 155)
Cornmeal
1 tablespoon halved and pitted brine-cured black olives, such as Kalamata
4 teaspoons grated Parmesan cheese

1. In a large nonstick skillet, combine the onion slices and the olive oil. Toss to coat the onions with the oil. Cover and cook over low heat, stirring occasionally, until the onions are tender, 5 to 7 minutes. Add the red pepper, raise the heat to medium-low and cook, stirring often, until the pepper strips are tender and the onions begin to brown, about 5 minutes. Season with the rosemary, salt and pepper. Remove from the heat and let cool slightly.

2. Preheat the oven to 425° F. Punch down the pizza dough and let rest 5 minutes. Sprinkle 2 baking sheets lightly with cornmeal. Divide the dough into 4 equal pieces. Shape each piece into a round disc and flatten with the palm of your hand. On a lightly floured board, roll out each piece into a 7-inch circle, lifting and turning the dough as you roll to stretch it gently.

3. Transfer the dough to the baking sheets, placing 2 circles on each. Spread the cooked onions and peppers over the rounds of dough, distributing evenly. Top with the black olives and sprinkle 1 teaspoon Parmesan cheese over each pizza.

4. Bake 15 to 20 minutes, until the bottom and edges of the crust are golden brown, switching the position of the baking sheets after 10 minutes. Let cool slightly before cutting each pizza into quarters to serve.

Mushroom, Green Pepper and Turkey Sausage Pizza

Fresh mushrooms, virtually fat-free and only 21 calories per cup raw, are a great choice for the health-conscious consumer. Turkey sausage keeps cholesterol down.

4 Servings — 397 Calories per serving

3 ounces Italian-style turkey sausage, casings removed, crumbled
1 teaspoon olive oil
10 ounces fresh mushrooms, thinly sliced
1 medium green bell pepper, cut into thin strips
¼ teaspoon salt
⅛ teaspoon freshly ground black pepper
1 recipe Pizza Dough (p. 155)
Cornmeal
½ cup Easy Marinara Sauce (p. 78) or your favorite bottled sauce
¼ cup shredded fat-free mozzarella (1 ounce)

1. Crumble the sausage into a large nonstick skillet and cook over medium heat, stirring and breaking up any lumps of meat with the side of a spatula, until well browned, about 10 minutes. With a slotted spoon, transfer the sausage to a dish.

2. Add the olive oil, mushrooms and pepper to the skillet. Cook over medium-low heat, stirring, until the vegetables are heated through, about 3 minutes. Cover and cook 3 minutes longer. Uncover, raise the heat to medium-high and cook, stirring, until the excess moisture evaporates and the mushrooms are lightly browned, about 5 minutes. Season with the salt and pepper.

3. Preheat the oven to 425° F. Punch down the pizza dough and let rest 5 minutes. Sprinkle 2 baking sheets lightly with cornmeal. Divide the dough into 4 equal pieces. Shape each piece into a round disc and flatten with the palm of your hand. On a lightly floured board, roll out each piece into a 7-inch circle, lifting and turning the dough as you roll to stretch it gently.

4. Transfer the dough to the prepared baking sheets, placing 2 circles on each. Spoon the mushroom and pepper mixture onto the pizzas, dividing evenly and spreading to the edges. Top with the cooked sausage and drizzle the tomato sauce over all. Sprinkle 1 tablespoon of the shredded mozzarella cheese over each pizza.

5. Bake 15 to 20 minutes, until the bottom and edges of the crust are golden brown, switching the position of the baking sheets after 10 minutes. Let cool slightly before cutting each pizza into quarters to serve.

Broccoli and Two-Cheese Pizza

Broccoli, America's favorite vegetable, is an excellent source of vitamin C, and it adds zero fat and only 23 calories to each of the following pizzas.

4 Servings — 398 Calories per serving

1 recipe Pizza Dough (p. 155)
Cornmeal
2 cups cooked broccoli florets
1 tablespoon slivered sun-dried tomatoes (about 4 halves)
6 ounces fat-free mozzarella cheese, coarsely shredded or cut into thin slices
4 teaspoons grated Parmesan cheese

1. Preheat the oven to 425° F. Punch down the pizza dough and let rest 5 minutes. Sprinkle 2 baking sheets lightly with cornmeal.

2. Divide the dough into 4 equal pieces. Shape each piece into a round disc and flatten with the palm of your hand. On a lightly floured board, roll out each piece into a 7-inch circle, lifting and turning the dough as you roll to stretch it gently.

3. Transfer the dough to the baking sheets, placing 2 circles on each. Arrange the broccoli on top, distributing evenly. Dot with the sun-dried tomatoes and sprinkle the mozzarella and Parmesan cheese evenly over the pizzas.

4. Bake 15 to 20 minutes, or until the edges of the crust are golden brown, switching the position of the baking sheets after 10 minutes. Let cool slightly before cutting each pizza into quarters to serve.

— *Fresh Tomato, Mozzarella and Basil Pizza* —

Basil, in season, adds a delicious fresh taste to this classic fresh tomato–topped pizza. In Italy this pizza is called "Margherita" after the much loved nineteenth-century Italian queen. When basil isn't in season use fresh Italian parsley instead.

4 Servings | 400 Calories per serving

1 recipe Pizza Dough (p. 155)
½ pound fat-free mozzarella cheese, coarsely shredded or cut into thin strips
2 tablespoons coarsely chopped fresh basil or Italian (flat-leaf) parsley
8 to 10 firm ripe plum tomatoes, thinly sliced Cornmeal

1. Preheat the oven to 425° F. Punch down the pizza dough and let rest 5 minutes. Sprinkle 2 baking sheets lightly with cornmeal.

2. Divide the dough into 4 equal pieces. Shape each piece into a round disc and flatten with the palm of your hand. On a lightly floured board, roll out each piece into a 7-inch circle, lifting and turning the dough as you roll to stretch it gently.

3. Transfer the dough to the baking sheets, placing 2 circles on each. Arrange the cheese on the top, dividing evenly. Sprinkle the basil over the pizzas. Arrange the tomato slices in a single even layer on top of the basil and cheese.

4. Bake 15 to 20 minutes, or until the edges of the crust are golden brown, switching the position of the baking sheets after 10 minutes. Let cool slightly before cutting each pizza into quarters to serve.

Red Onion and Thyme Focaccia

MAKES 24 PIECES | 55 CALORIES PER PIECE

1 tablespoon plus 2 teaspoons olive oil
¼ cup finely chopped red onion plus 1 cup thinly sliced red onion
1 cup lukewarm water (105° F. to 115° F.)
1 tablespoon active dry yeast
1½ to 2 cups unbleached all-purpose flour
½ cup whole wheat flour
½ plus ⅛ teaspoon salt
¼ teaspoon coarsely ground black pepper
Cornmeal
1 teaspoon fresh thyme or ½ teaspoon dried

1. In a small skillet, heat 1 tablespoon of the olive oil. Add the chopped red onion and cook over medium-low heat, stirring often, until golden, about 5 minutes. Remove from the heat and let cool.

2. In a large bowl, combine the warm water and yeast. Cover with plastic wrap and let stand until the yeast is dissolved, about 5 minutes. Add 1½ cups of the all-purpose flour, the whole wheat flour, the ½ teaspoon of salt, the pepper and the cooked chopped onion with its oil. Stir until blended. Gradually add enough of the remaining flour to form a soft dough.

3. Turn out onto a lightly floured board and knead, adding as much of the remaining flour as needed to prevent sticking, until the dough is smooth and springs back when pressed, about 5 minutes. Form the dough into a ball and place in a clean large bowl; brush the surface lightly with a little olive oil. Cover with plastic wrap and let stand in a warm place until doubled in bulk, about 1½ hours.

4. Meanwhile, in a large nonstick skillet, combine the sliced red onion with the remaining 2 teaspoons olive oil. Cover and cook over low heat, stirring occasionally, until the onion is soft but not brown, about 20 minutes. Uncover and cook, stirring, just to cook off any moisture, about 2 minutes. Set aside to cool.

5. Preheat the oven to 425° F. When the dough is ready, punch it down and let rest 5 minutes. Sprinkle a large baking sheet lightly with cornmeal. On a lightly floured board, roll out the dough, turning and stretching it gently, into a rectangle about 14 × 10 inches. Transfer to the baking sheet. Spread the cooked onions over the dough. Season with the thyme, salt and an additional grinding of pepper.

6. Bake the focaccia until the bottom and edges are well browned, about 15 minutes. Let cool slightly before cutting into small squares. Serve warm or at room temperature.

Rosemary and Garlic Focaccia

MAKES 24 PIECES | 58 CALORIES PER PIECE

1 cup lukewarm water (105° F. to 115° F.)
2 teaspoons sugar
2 teaspoons active dry yeast
2 tablespoons olive oil
2 to 2½ cups unbleached all-purpose flour
1½ teaspoons dried rosemary
½ teaspoon salt
1 tablespoon finely chopped garlic
Cornmeal

1. In a large bowl, combine the warm water, sugar and yeast. Cover with plastic wrap and let stand until the yeast is dissolved, about 5 minutes. Add 1 tablespoon of the olive oil, 2 cups of the flour, 1 teaspoon of the rosemary and the salt. Stir until blended. Gradually add enough of the remaining flour to form a soft dough.

2. Turn out onto a lightly floured board and knead, adding as much of the remaining flour as needed to prevent sticking, until the dough is smooth and springs back when pressed with your fingertip, about 5 minutes. Form the dough into a ball and place in a large clean bowl. Brush the surface lightly with a little olive oil. Cover with plastic wrap and let stand in a warm place until doubled in bulk, about 1½ hours.

3. Meanwhile, in a small skillet, combine the remaining 1 tablespoon olive oil and the garlic. Cook over medium-low heat, stirring, until the garlic is softened and fragrant but not brown, about 3 minutes. Remove from the heat and let cool.

4. Preheat the oven to 425° F. When the dough is ready, punch it down and let rest 5 minutes. Sprinkle a large baking sheet lightly with cornmeal. Roll out the dough, turning and stretching it gently, into a rectangle about 15 × 10 inches. Transfer to the baking sheet. Spread the garlic mixture over the dough. Sprinkle the remaining ½ teaspoon rosemary on top.

5. Bake the focaccia until the bottom and edges are well browned, about 15 minutes. Let cool slightly before cutting into small squares. Serve warm or at room temperature.

Grilled Chicken, Zucchini and Red Pepper Panino

Who would think you could afford a double-crust sandwich while watching your waistline? This one, loaded with chicken and vegetables, would make a most satisfying lunch.

MAKES 1 SANDWICH — 391 CALORIES

1 teaspoon olive oil
½ garlic clove, crushed through a press
1 small zucchini (about 3 ounces), cut lengthwise into thin slices
1 skinless, boneless chicken breast half (3½ ounces)
Salt and freshly ground black pepper
1 teaspoon red wine vinegar
½ roasted medium red bell pepper (p. 24), cut into strips, or use ¼ cup jarred roasted red pepper strips
4-inch piece of Italian bread, halved lengthwise
1 teaspoon chopped fresh basil (optional)

1. Place the olive oil and garlic on a plate; stir with a fork to blend. Rub a little on the zucchini slices. Add the chicken breast to the plate and turn to coat both sides with the remaining garlic oil.

2. Light a hot fire in a grill or heat a nonstick skillet over medium heat until hot enough to evaporate a drop of water. Add the zucchini and grill or cook, turning, until evenly browned, 3 to 5 minutes on a grill, 2 to 3 minutes in the skillet. Set aside. Grill or sauté the chicken breast, turning until evenly browned and cooked through, about 5 minutes per side on the grill, 3 minutes per side in the skillet. Season the chicken with salt and pepper to taste. Sprinkle the vinegar over the chicken, zucchini and red pepper strips.

3. On the grill, under the broiler or in a toaster, toast the cut sides of the bread until golden. Layer the red pepper, zucchini slices and chicken on the toasted bread. Sprinkle the basil on top. Using a serrated knife, cut the sandwich in half diagonally and serve.

– Spinach, Mozzarella and Sweet Onion Panino –

Perfect for a picnic, this cheese and vegetable hero is packed with flavor in every bite.

MAKES 1 SANDWICH — 388 CALORIES

4-inch piece of whole wheat Italian bread, halved lengthwise
½ cup shredded fat-free mozzarella cheese (1½ ounces)
½ cup fresh steamed or thawed frozen spinach, well squeezed
½ teaspoon extra virgin olive oil
½ teaspoon red wine vinegar
2 thin slices of sweet yellow onion, separated into rings
2 small sun-dried tomato halves packed in oil, cut into thin slivers

1. Preheat your broiler. Set both bread slices, cut sides up, on a small baking sheet. Sprinkle the shredded mozzarella cheese over the bottom half of the bread. Broil about 6 inches from the heat until the cheese is melted and bubbly and the other piece of bread is toasted, 1 to 2 minutes.

2. In a small bowl, toss the cooked spinach with the olive oil and vinegar. Spread the spinach on the toasted side of the bread. Arrange the onion rings over the spinach and sprinkle the slivers of sun-dried tomato on top. Place the two halves of the bread together and using a serrated knife, cut in half diagonally. Serve while the melted cheese is still warm.

Chapter Eight

DOLCI—ITALIAN DESSERTS

In Italian, the word *dolci* means sweets, and that is what is used to describe what we call dessert. Rich pastries, for which Italian bakeries are famous, are usually reserved for late afternoon or a midmorning espresso break. After a large meal, a pear, an apple, a bunch of grapes or an orange, with perhaps a bowl of walnuts and a sliver of Parmesan or Gorgonzola cheese, would be the ending of choice. In Italy, at the end of a meal, a bowl of perfectly ripened seasonal fruit is more typical than a pastry cart overflowing with gooey desserts.

The most exquisite dessert I ever experienced was in a restaurant in Florence on a hot, dusty August afternoon. After a substantial lunch we were each served a large glass bowl of dark red cherries floating in iced water. The sensations of sweet and icy cold were sublime. It never occurred to me at the time that it was a "healthy dessert."

While dessert in Italy usually means fruit, it might be fresh (a platter of grapes, apples and bananas), poached or baked. Of course, the advantage of these kinds of desserts for dieters is that most of them can be almost totally free of fat and subsequently lower in calories.

In addition to fruit desserts, I have included a cake, or *torta*, and cookies, or *biscotti,* both of which are marvelous with a good strong cup of Italian espresso. Pignoli Macaroons are chewy, with just the right amount of sweetness, and the moist and elegant Walnut and Orange Torta, perfect in size for entertaining, is made with olive oil instead of butter. And no, you don't taste the olive oil in the cake.

Frozen desserts are also a good choice for a sweet treat. While Italians love their rich ice cream, *gelato,* as much as we do, they also specialize in deeply flavored frozen ices, *granite,* which are ideal for light dining. Unlike a sherbert, a *granita* has a coarse, crystalline, rather than smooth, texture. *Granite* make wonderfully refreshing endings to large meals, and they are marvelous as a snack on a hot summer afternoon.

Since each of these desserts adds up to 250 calories or less, even if you are dining on the light side, you will surely be able to find room for that little something sweet whenever you are in the mood. In fact, a number of the Italian ices hover around 100 calories, and several dip well below, to allow you not only an after-dinner dessert, but a sweet fix from time to time.

Cherries in Red Wine

Serve this intensely flavored dessert ice cold. It is pretty when served in stemmed glasses, topped with a spoonful of low-fat vanilla yogurt instead of whipped cream.

6 SERVINGS 188 CALORIES PER SERVING

1½ pounds dark sweet cherries, stemmed and pitted
2 cups full-flavored dry red wine, such as Chianti Classico
½ vanilla bean or ½ teaspoon vanilla extract (see Note)
¾ cup sugar
6 tablespoons low-fat vanilla yogurt

1. In a large nonaluminum saucepan, combine the cherries, wine, vanilla bean and sugar. Heat over medium heat until boiling. Reduce the heat to low and simmer, uncovered, 20 minutes.

2. Remove the vanilla bean from the poached cherries; split it lengthwise in half and using the tip of a small knife, scrape out the vanilla seeds. Add the vanilla seeds to the cherries; discard the pod.

3. Using a slotted spoon, transfer about 1 cup of the poached cherries to a food processor and purée. Return the purée to the cherries in the saucepan. Let the mixture cool. Transfer to a bowl and refrigerate until very cold, at least 2 hours.

4. To serve, divide the cherries and wine syrup among 6 dessert glasses and top each with 1 tablespoon of yogurt. Serve ice cold.

NOTE *If using vanilla extract, stir it into the saucepan along with the purée in step 3.*

Cantaloupe with White Wine and Cinnamon

Any sweet coral- or orange-fleshed melon from the muskmelon family can be used for this recipe. The sweetness of the melon will balance the acidity of the wine and the slight heat of the spicy cinnamon adds just the right counterpoint.

4 SERVINGS — 110 CALORIES PER SERVING

2 small or 1 large ripe cantaloupe
1 cup fruity white wine, such as Trebbiano or Soave
½ teaspoon ground cinnamon

1. Cut the cantaloupe in half. Scoop out the seeds and cut each half into 4 wedges. Cut off the outer rind.

2. Arrange the cantaloupe in a large shallow bowl or on a deep platter. Pour the wine over the melon. Sprinkle lightly with the ground cinnamon.

3. Cover with plastic wrap and refrigerate 1 hour, or just long enough to chill the melon slightly.

Orange, Grapefruit and Grapes with Campari

Campari is a popular Italian bitters with a beautiful cherry-red color. The flavor is bittersweet and it is especially refreshing when mixed with soda and served over ice. Here it adds spark and sophistication to a pleasant combination of citrus fruits and green grapes.

4 Servings | 137 Calories per serving

2 large seedless navel oranges, skin and white pith removed, cut into sections
1 large pink grapefruit, skin and white pith removed, cut into sections, seeds removed
1 cup seedless green grapes
¼ cup Campari
Sugar, to taste

1. In a serving bowl, combine the oranges, grapefruit and green grapes. Add the Campari. Cover with plastic wrap and refrigerate, tossing occasionally, until ready to serve.

2. Serve with sugar on the side for those who prefer a slightly sweeter dessert. Each teaspoon of sugar will add 16 calories.

Baked Peaches with Almonds

Instead of butter, this recipe uses light-flavored pure olive oil as the fat. Baked peaches are a popular Tuscan dessert. Top these with a dollop of low-fat yogurt, if you like, at an extra 9 calories per tablespoon.

8 Servings — 141 Calories per serving

4 large firm ripe peaches, preferably freestone
½ cup packed light brown sugar
2 tablespoons all-purpose flour
½ teaspoon ground cinnamon
2 tablespoons pure olive oil
¼ cup sliced unblanched almonds

1. Preheat the oven to 350° F. Lightly oil a 9 × 13-inch baking dish.

2. Bring a saucepan half filled with water to a boil. Add the peaches and boil about 1 minute. Drain and cool the peaches under cold running water. Peel off the skins. Halve the peaches and remove the pits. Arrange the peaches, cut sides up, in the baking dish.

3. In a small bowl, combine the brown sugar, flour and cinnamon; stir to mix. Add the olive oil and blend with your fingertips or a fork until crumbly. Sprinkle the crumbs and the almonds over the peaches.

4. Bake 25 to 30 minutes, or until the crumbs are golden. Serve warm or at room temperature.

Poached Peaches

Use perfectly ripened peaches at the height of the season. Freestone are my personal favorite. Boiling the fruit for just a minute loosens the skins and makes them easy to peel.

4 Servings — 230 Calories per serving

4 medium firm, ripe peaches, preferably freestone
¾ cup plus 2 tablespoons sugar

1 cinnamon stick
1 strip of orange zest (2 × 1/2 inch)
1 tablespoon fresh lemon juice
4 fresh mint leaves, for garnish

1. Bring a medium saucepan of water to a boil. Add the peaches and boil 1 minute. Drain and cool the peaches under cold running water. Peel off the skins. Halve the peaches and remove the pits.

2. In a large wide saucepan or Dutch oven, combine the sugar with 2 cups of water. Bring to a boil over medium heat, stirring until the sugar dissolves, about 5 minutes. Add the cinnamon stick and orange zest and boil gently, uncovered, until the syrup is slightly thickened, about 15 minutes.

3. Add the peaches, reduce the heat to low and poach 10 minutes, or until the peaches are tender. Remove from the heat. Add the lemon juice and let the peaches cool in the liquid. Cover and refrigerate until very cold, at least 2 hours or up to a day.

4. Serve in shallow dessert bowls. Garnish each serving with a mint leaf.

Pears Baked with Honey and Nutmeg

4 Servings — 215 Calories per serving

4 large medium-ripe pears
2 teaspoons butter, cut into 8 small pieces
2 tablespoons fresh lemon juice
4 tablespoons honey
1 teaspoon grated lemon zest
1/4 teaspoon ground nutmeg
4 tablespoons plain low-fat yogurt

1. Preheat the oven to 350° F. Halve the pears and with a teaspoon, scoop out the cores. Arrange the pears, cut sides up, in a 9 × 13-inch baking dish.

2. Place a piece of butter in each pear half. Drizzle the lemon juice and honey over the pears, distributing evenly. Sprinkle with the lemon zest and the nutmeg.

3. Bake, basting frequently with the juices, 35 to 40 minutes, or until the pears are golden. Serve warm or at room temperature. Top each serving with 1 tablespoon yogurt.

Pears with Sweetened Ricotta

Very ripe, sweet pears are the secret to this simple, but tasty dessert. Make the ricotta mixture up ahead of time, but halve and peel the pears just before serving or else they will turn brown.

4 Servings | 93 Calories per serving

½ cup reduced-fat or part-skim ricotta cheese
1 tablespoon confectioners' sugar
2 tablespoons milk, half-and-half or heavy cream
½ teaspoon grated lemon zest
2 large ripe pears, preferably Bartlett
1½ tablespoons fresh lemon juice
Grated nutmeg

1. In a medium bowl, combine the ricotta cheese, confectioners' sugar, milk and lemon zest. Whisk until the mixture is light. Cover with plastic wrap and refrigerate until serving time.

2. Just before serving, halve the pears and with a teaspoon, scoop out the cores. Sprinkle with the lemon juice and arrange the pears on dessert plates.

3. Heap about 2 tablespoons of the ricotta filling on each pear half, dividing evenly. Dust with grated nutmeg and serve.

Plum Granita

Granita is the Italian version of the French *sorbet.* The name comes from the word *grana,* which means grain and best describes the characteristically coarse, grainy texture of the frozen dessert. This texture is a result of the frequent stirring the mixture of fruit juice, water and sugar syrup undergoes while it is freezing.

Traditionally granita is made with a simple syrup and a fruit purée. In order to hasten the chilling time for this recipe I have combined the sugar, fruit and half the water in the first step and quickly cooled the whole mixture by using ice cubes for the remaining portion of the water. This cuts the freezing time almost in half.

4 SERVINGS — 155 CALORIES PER SERVING

1 pound juicy ripe red plums (6 or 7)
½ cup sugar
1 cup water
1 tray (12 or 14) ice cubes

1. Working over a medium saucepan to catch the juices, halve the plums and remove and discard the pits. Cut the plums into large chunks and put them in the saucepan. Add the sugar and water and bring to a boil over medium heat, stirring to dissolve the sugar. Cover and cook 5 minutes, or until the plums are soft. Remove from the heat.

2. Working in 2 batches, purée half of the plum mixture and half of the ice cubes in a food processor or blender. Repeat with the remaining plums and ice cubes. Pour into a 9 × 13-inch baking pan and place in the freezer.

3. Freeze, stirring the slushy center into the almost-frozen edges with a fork every 20 minutes, until the mixture is evenly frozen, 1 to 2 hours.

4. To serve, spoon the granita into wine glasses or goblets. If it gets too hard, soften slightly in the refrigerator about 20 minutes and shave off portions with the side of an ice cream scoop or large spoon.

Lemon Granita

Lemon granita is simple and straightforward—an Italian classic. This recipe can also be made with freshly squeezed pink grapefruit juice or with fresh lime juice.

6 Servings | 107 Calories per serving

2 cups water
3/4 cup sugar
1 cup freshly squeezed lemon juice, strained

1. In a small nonaluminum saucepan, combine the water and sugar. Bring to a boil over medium heat, stirring to dissolve the sugar, about 5 minutes. Remove from the heat and let cool. (The syrup can be made 1 to 2 days ahead and stored in the refrigerator until ready to use.)

2. Add the lemon juice to the sugar syrup and pour into a 9 × 13-inch baking pan. Freeze, stirring the slushy center into the almost-frozen edges with a fork every 20 minutes, until the mixture is evenly frozen, 1 to 2 hours.

3. To serve, scoop the granita into wine glasses or goblets. If it gets too hard, soften slightly in the refrigerator about 20 minutes and shave off portions with the side of an ice cream scoop or large spoon.

Strawberry Granita

The flavor of the strawberries is very important to this recipe. Out-of-season, frozen unsweetened strawberries are often a better choice than the large tasteless berries imported from foreign climes.

6 Servings | 75 Calories per serving

1 1/2 cups water
1/3 cup sugar
2 pints strawberries, hulled and sliced (about 6 cups)
1 tablespoon fresh lime or lemon juice

1. In a small nonaluminum saucepan, combine the water and sugar. Bring to a boil over medium heat, stirring until the sugar is dissolved, about 5 minutes. Remove from the heat and let cool. (The syrup can be made 1 to 2 days ahead and stored in the refrigerator until ready to use.)

2. Purée the strawberries and about ½ cup of the syrup in a food processor. Press the purée through a large strainer—not a fine mesh sieve—set over a bowl to remove the seeds. Stir the remaining syrup and the lime juice into the strawberry purée.

3. Pour the mixture into a 9 × 13-inch baking pan and freeze, stirring the slushy center into the almost-frozen edges with a fork every 20 minutes, until the mixture is evenly frozen, 1 to 2 hours.

4. To serve, scoop the granita into dessert bowls or goblets. If it gets too hard, soften slightly in the refrigerator about 20 minutes and shave off portions with the side of an ice cream scoop or large spoon.

Cafe Latte Granita

This tastes like iced espresso that has been sweetened with sugar and flavored with milk. It provides a refreshing finale to a sophisticated meal with surprisingly few calories.

8 Servings — 58 Calories per serving

2 cups strong, freshly brewed espresso
⅓ to ½ cup sugar, to taste
1 to 1½ cups low-fat milk, to taste

1. In a medium bowl, combine the espresso and sugar. Stir until the sugar is dissolved. Add the milk and stir to blend.

2. Pour into a 9 × 13-inch baking pan and freeze, stirring the slushy center into the almost-frozen edges with a fork every 20 minutes, until the mixture is evenly frozen, 1 to 2 hours. If it gets too hard, soften slightly in the refrigerator about 20 minutes and shave off portions with the side of an ice cream scoop or large spoon.

3. To serve, scoop the granita into dessert bowls or wine glasses.

Frulati di Frutta

Frulati di frutta, or fruit whip, is an iced beverage that is served as a popular snack in sidewalk cafes throughout Italy. I find it a tasty, not overly rich way to end a meal.

1 Serving — 162 Calories per serving

1 cup hulled sliced strawberries, or peeled sliced banana or peaches and/ or nectarines
2/3 cup low-fat milk
1 tablespoon sugar
1/4 cup cracked ice cubes

1. In a blender or food processor, combine the fruit of choice, milk, sugar and ice cubes. Blend 1 to 2 minutes, stirring as needed to mix the ingredients, until the ice and fruit are puréed.

2. Pour into a tall glass and serve with a straw and a long-handled spoon.

Oranges with White Zinfandel and Cinnamon

4 Servings — 124 Calories per serving

4 large seedless navel oranges
1 teaspoon sugar
1 cup chilled white zinfandel wine
Ground cinnamon

1. Using a sharp knife, cut the orange rind and white pith from the oranges. Cut the oranges into round slices about 1/4 inch thick.

2. Arrange the orange rounds in slightly overlapping concentric circles on a deep serving platter. Sprinkle the sugar over the oranges and drizzle on the wine. Sprinkle lightly with cinnamon.

3. Cover the oranges with plastic wrap and refrigerate until well chilled, at least 1 hour, before serving. Serve on dessert plates with a knife and fork.

Pignoli Macaroons

These chewy little wafers are wonderful served with a bowl of granita, a cup of espresso or a glass of dessert wine. Buy the pignoli in bulk in health food or specialty food shops.

MAKES ABOUT 2½ DOZEN | 42 CALORIES PER COOKIE

3 ounces (about ¾ cup) pignoli (pine nuts)
½ cup sugar
1 package (3.5 ounces) marzipan (almond paste)
1 egg white
½ teaspoon vanilla extract

1. Finely grind ½ cup of the pignoli and the sugar in a food processor. Cut the marzipan into ½-inch chunks. With the processor running, add a few chunks of the marzipan at a time through the feed tube. Process until thoroughly blended.

2. In a small bowl, lightly whisk the egg white with the vanilla until foamy. With the processor running, add the egg white to the sugar mixture. Transfer the pastelike mixture to a dinner plate and spread into a smooth layer. Let stand, uncovered, at room temperature until it is no longer sticky to the touch.

3. Preheat the oven to 350° F. Line 2 baking sheets with aluminum foil. Wetting your fingers continually with cold water to prevent sticking, shape small portions of the paste into ½-inch balls. Place on the baking sheets, leaving at least 2 inches between each ball. Press a pinch of the remaining pignoli into the top of each ball of paste, about 6 pignoli per cookie.

4. Bake 1 sheet at a time on a rack positioned in the middle of the oven 10 to 12 minutes, or until the edges are lightly browned.

5. Let the cookies set and cool before removing them from the sheets; carefully peel the cookies from the aluminum foil. The bottoms should be as smooth as glass and the foil will peel right off. Store the cookies, uncovered, so they will remain slightly crunchy.

Walnut and Orange Torta

This flat, European-style cake is unusual in that it is made with olive oil rather than butter. While the calories are the same, 120 calories per tablespoon, olive oil contains no cholesterol. The use of egg whites in place of whole eggs also limits saturated fat while reducing calories. Be sure to choose a lightly flavored olive oil for this dessert, or another tasteless vegetable oil.

14 Servings — 250 Calories per serving

1 whole egg, at room temperature
3 egg whites, at room temperature
1 cup granulated sugar
Juice and grated zest of 1 orange (1/3 cup juice and 1 tablespoon grated zest)
1 teaspoon vanilla extract
3/4 cup lightly flavored olive oil or other light vegetable oil
1 cup all-purpose flour
1 cup finely ground walnuts
1 teaspoon baking powder
2 tablespoons confectioners' sugar, for dusting

1. Preheat the oven to 350° F. Lightly oil and flour a 10-inch springform pan.

2. In a large mixer bowl, beat the whole egg and egg whites on high speed until light in color, about 5 minutes. Gradually beat in the granulated sugar until the mixture is foamy, pale yellow and increased in volume, about 5 minutes longer. On low speed, gradually beat in the orange juice, orange zest and vanilla. Beat in the olive oil in a slow steady stream until blended.

3. In a separate bowl, combine the flour, walnuts and baking powder; stir to mix. Add to the egg mixture and gently fold together until blended. Pour into the prepared springform pan.

4. Bake 30 to 35 minutes, or until the edges of the torta begin to pull away from the sides of the pan. Let cool on a wire rack. Run a narrow spatula around the edge of the pan to loosen the cake and remove the sides of the pan. Let cool completely. Dust the top of the cake with the confectioners' sugar before cutting it into thin wedges to serve.

INDEX